A Time for Being Human

A Time for Being Human

EUGENE KENNEDY

IMAGE BOOKS
A DIVISION OF DOUBLEDAY & COMPANY, INC.
GARDEN CITY, NEW YORK
1987

Image Books edition published March 1987 by special arrangement with The Thomas More Press.

Library of Congress Cataloging-in-Publication Data

Kennedy, Eugene C.
  A time for being human.

  Reprint. Originally published: Chicago: Thomas More Press, c1977.
  1. Meditations. I. Title.
[BX2182.2.K427 1987]   242   86-20936
ISBN 0-385-23538-0 (pbk.)

For Eppie

Contents

CHAPTER 3

And a time to die . . .

CHAPTER 4

A time to plant and a time to uproot the plant . . .

CHAPTER 5

**A time to kill and a time to heal
A time to tear down and a time to build up . . .**

CHAPTER 6

**A time to weep and a time to laugh
A time to mourn and a time to dance . . .**

CHAPTER 7

A time to scatter stones and a time to gather them
A time to embrace and a time to be far from embraces . . .

CHAPTER 8

A time to seek and a time to lose
A time to keep and a time to cast away . . .

CHAPTER 9

A time to rend and a time to sew
A time to be silent and a time to speak . . .

Contents

Introduction

There comes a moment to everyone, wrote dramatist Edmund Rostand, "when beauty stands staring into the soul with sad, sweet eyes that sicken at the sound of words. And God help those who pass the moment by." This is a book about such moments, about instants and pauses and turning points, about the intervals and sideways glances that permit us the opportunity and just the right angle of vision to see clearly what we so often search for fruitlessly—meaning in life. This is a book about the times of our lives, a collection of reflections and meditations generated by glimpses—some no longer in duration than the smallest fraction of a moment—in which something of the goodness and truth of existence, some hint of all that, in Joyce's phrase, is "grave and constant" about our human situation may suddenly be seen. We hardly ever see these things if we look for them; we are too self-conscious, too weighty in our philosophical resolve, too determined, like a posturing preacher, to impose rather than to discover meaning.

It is the special burden of those who must preserve any kind of orthodoxy that they must always trace things back from the conclusions to which they have already come. They know how the story or the meditation, yes, and even the idle musing, must come out and this certainty of vision leaves them no room for anything but journeys as straight and direct as the straight line drawn swiftly between any two points. Ah, but the journey is finally the thing, the special pilgrimage characterized more by leisure than haste, on which we find the world and ourselves and a harvest of glorious small hints about our nature and purpose. The adventure built on departing from the direct route to our destination takes us into territory that is both simple and grand, under sputtering cataracts and across shadowed valleys, through a thousand griefs to the mountaintop of joy. One need not deny or subvert orthodoxy to state that only varied journeys toward it permit us to understand its finely marbled consistency. If it is wisdom, it is an amalgam of the richest of human ores fired twice in the blaze of our common suffering, a purified symbol of all our achievement and failure.

There are times when we can see ourselves, and recognize the heroic cast of our condition. The greatest and the most powerful share the same longings and hopes as the least noted and most vulnerable among us. There are times for gathering and scattering, for living and dying, for loving and healing. The thoughts of this book fit roughly into these seasons of our passage. None of them fits perfectly despite the source of their inspiration in incidents that by themselves would fit better. That is part of the mystery of our pilgrimage on which things so often go wrong, and only afterward do we recognize the truths we were gazing at but did not comprehend along the way. Time is indeed out of joint for most human beings; how strange—but how common—that at our greatest moments, at a wedding, a graduation, an anniversary celebration, we do not feel quite the way we expected or hoped we would. How common for us to see it all better, and savor it more, in retrospect; that is why our recollections get better as time moves on. We smooth out the rough spots and fill in the missing places; we see the essence of the event in better perspective. But that integration of experience is only achieved later on if, despite our hurry, we can see into the moments of ordinary time that can go screaming through our hands like a fisherman's line taken by a shark. This is a book for the times that count, for the times we must collect and preserve in order to possess our lives in peace and joy.

One of our most abiding frustrations is built on the expectation that someday the right time will arrive for us, the time when we will not be in a hurry, or when we will be able to enjoy the moments of existence with sufficient shield for our own vulnerability to illness, loss, or disappointment. The time will come, we promise ourselves in a corner of our souls, when we will be safe with the best of our treasures, with integrity and faith and love, in some place where they will no longer be constantly tested. But, of course, that moment has already arrived; we sense the richness of life under pressure and strain, when we respond rather than when we relax. We are most alive when we actively believe, when we keep investing in hope, when we must reach steadily out to others in love. There is no rest for the weary, the old saying goes, but it deserves an amendment—for there is truly no rest for the lively. The time is always wrong and the time is always right for being human, for inhabiting fully the gift of life that God has given us. Reflection and meditation are our best means of living these experiences deeply—and of possessing them so that they can never be taken away—in their very occurrence.

Yet there are those who prefer an abstract meditation on an intellectualized God in a crystalline palace of a heaven, on a God who would have us close our eyes to the glorious imperfection of the world and of each other. Indeed, as these words are written, the movement back to a spirituality of other-worldliness has regrouped in significant numbers, buoyed by new recruits, and seems set on storming the heights of supernatural withdrawal once again. The temptation to think that the time is right for that is difficult to resist; it is easier in many ways to reject a hurting world than it is to embrace it with compassion. It is easier to think harshly than tenderly about the complexities of the human situation. The time has never been worse for such a retreat; it is, if anything, a rejection of God's free gifts, a failure of sacramental vision, a proof of timidity about entering the future. And in the long run, such an escape from the face of reality will cause more suffering than it will cure.

The time—the Scriptures echo it over and over again—is now. The marvels of creation are strewn about us in the moments of every day, in the invisible bonds, now slack and now drawn taut, of our relationships with each other, and in the simple and unending tests of our strength that we feel through these every day. Now is the time, even though the time does not and never will seem right, now is the time to affirm and so lay hold of the humanity that the super-spiritual disdain even when God does not. This is a book about everything simple and grand, everything that does not quite fit together that finally forms a unity, about the homeland of ordinary events in which are revealed all our mysteries.

Eugene Kennedy

CHAPTER 1

There is a season for everything . . .

On time . . .

Time, despite its elusive essence, preoccupies us. We either seem to have too much of it or not enough. We are pressed to buy it as well as to spend it, to kill it as well as to save it; it can be lost but it can also be found. Time, Pythagoras was supposed to have said, is the soul of the world. It has been heralded as a friend and described as an enemy. A great phrase booms out of the Scriptures, like the hour being sounded on a clock: *Now* is the time, *now* is the hour of salvation.

In an era that has been marked by a change of time in order to save the light at the end of the day, it is worthwhile to reflect on time and its many meanings for all of us.

Changing time . . .

There are many experiences when, for an instant at least, we seem to escape time itself and gaze into a world where it can neither touch nor intimidate us. This may happen when, gazing at a work of art, we suddenly understand that the human experience of a long-dead artist is co-extensive with our own and how, in a fashion beyond understanding, we stand together in a dimension that cannot be measured by clocks or calendars. This is why you cannot rush through an art gallery or speed-read through the masterpieces of literature. We must be willing to submerge ourselves in time in order to transform it in a lasting way. This also requires that we surrender ourselves to our experience of the world, that we lower our defenses against our own feelings and against the hurts or misunderstandings as well as the happinesses that we have known in life. We cannot survive or understand the meaning of time without these moments.

Using time this way is like dreaming while we are awake. Just as dreams have a special function of integrating our experiences while we sleep, allowing ourselves time for contemplation is indispensable to a completed sense of our own identity. Contemplation places us at the edge of wonder, enabling us to always see things freshly and with an appreciation that challenges the grindstones of boredom. We cannot, however, develop a sense of wonder unless we loosen our grip on time, unless we surrender to its flow and allow the sands of time to run through our fingers. This is an important part of becoming human.

There is, in other words, a successful way of losing time, an experience that does not imperil us but that enriches us. People are forever worrying about lost time, about moments that they did not use well or through which they slept or in which they did not pay enough attention to themselves or the other people in their lives. As Anne Morrow Lindbergh once wrote: "Lost time is like a run in a stocking. It always gets worse." We may never understand time if we are preoccupied with filling it in a puritanical and utilitarian fashion. Time that is lost is not necessarily time that is wasted. As we feel free enough to lose time in wonder and contemplation, we lay hold of its meaning and are able to employ it more significantly afterward.

If we watch our time the way an accountant watches the books, we may never be able to freely give away any of our time or ourselves. We may be oppressed with a sense that every bit of time must be accounted for down to the last second. God did not create the universe this way or intend for his creatures to live in this manner. As we learn to lose time through giving it up to others, we discover something timeless about life itself.

Some people find it more difficult to give of their time than of their money. They would like to buy a kind of privacy that saves them from the need to respond to a world that always makes its demands at such inopportune times. A husband and wife, in a fundamental learning about love, must be able to give of their time to each other; this enables them to enter into time together. The demands they make on each other frequently come when they have little time to give. If only these things could be put off until tomorrow! Things of the heart can never be delayed, however, and as we are willing to lose our own time for the sake of each other, we discover something that we can never afterward lose at all—the found time that comes when people look at each other with love and concern.

On meditation

What does modern meditation promise? It is not without its pledges, for it has become as marketable as popular drugs and its enticements are similar to theirs: relief, not for indigestion or for insomnia, but for the woes of life, for the travail of the human condition. Meditation, in many of its contemporary forms, offers a pathway out of the noise of existence, a journey to "tranquillity base" that is as soundless as that moon encampment was for the astronauts. Meditation is presented as a sedative rather than a stimulant—a means to close gently, rather than open wide, the doors of perception.

But is that the point? Perhaps it is, especially of certain forms of meditation from the Far East. But should we choose this as the port of call for Western man? Or does floating in the silent sea or in a timeless, stone-filled garden have the appeal that all distant things do for busy twentieth-century persons? These forms of meditation do allow us to discover something more about ourselves. They make it possible for us to contemplate ourselves, and many of us find this endlessly fascinating and entertaining. They are not even disturbed by reminders of Narcissus and the pool that received his gaze.

Can we be sure that when we wash up on these islands of solitude we will be enlarged by the experience? Or is there some danger that our fascination with ourselves will build impacted self-absorption? Does meditation lead us more into ourselves or does it break us open to life? It could go either way, but it is clear that the feature of much of contemporary meditation is a snuggling into one's own psyche. The soul thus embraced becomes a hideaway from the self rather than an arena of hospitality for others. Does meditation mean that we are the only guests we can be sure of in our inner space?

There seems to be a longing for exile, for an austere and quiet life, although it is recognized that this is a vocation for a select few. And even the monks make bread while most people have to make do the best way they can in a clanging, hurried civilization. But cannot the city be a focus of meditation as much as the country? Is not humanity revealed there as well as anyplace else? Must we go far away in order to more clearly see ourselves up close? There is no small confusion about this at the present time, and it is not helped by the emphasis on meditation as a form of treatment for nerves that jangle like a tin mobile in the wind. Is meditation, after all, meant to be a cure or something that makes us more sensitive to our ills?

We must ask what else meditation might be in the Judeo-Christian tradition. Well, we might answer, anything but an escape from life. It is true that prophets and the priests have always gone out to the desert, but they never stayed there except in very small numbers. Most persons retreat to solitude in order to get a better vision of the city to which they must return, to see more deeply into the life they cannot leave without deserting their most fundamental responsibilities and commitments.

Out of the desert have I called you, we read, knowing that the place of retreat is a luxury we long for but which we cannot always afford. A meditative journey to the desert offers us a way of locating ourselves in time and space, but it does not offer us a way out of time and space. It makes us more intensely aware of the dimensions in existence rather than numbing us to them. Meditation does not cloak but reveals reality and our relationship to our specific place and set of relationships in it. We enter the veil of contemplation not to escape these realities but to discover them.

Meditation also provides us with a way of relating better to ourselves because it gives us time to listen to ourselves and to hear what we are saying and feeling about life. It offers us the opportunity to forgive ourselves and to come close to our own personalities, so that we are not always living at a distance from the heart of our own being. It enables us to be ourselves, loving ourselves more truthfully and making it possible, then, for us to love others with this more truly realized self of our own.

There is no way that human beings can gain greater possession of themselves and come closer to other persons without at the same time becoming more aware of their relationship to God. This is obviously one of the traditional functions of meditation, but it is not something to lull us to sleep in the arms of God as much as it is to place us into an active and loving relationship with him.

Meditation offers us the opportunity to consolidate our experience, to let things come together so that we can see the meaning of what we have been through and appreciate the direction of our days and the overall shape of our lives. Meditation is a precious time for plotting the movement of our own stars. It is one of the means through which we come more fully to inhabit our own identity.

Meditation, then, is anything but a sedative. It is not a narcotic offering the rest of sleep. Contemplation provides a time in which we minimize distractions so that we can take a long and unblinking look at the tragic face of existence. Reflection allows us to acquaint ourselves with infirmity. Meditation offers us the opportunity to look carefully at what we are tempted to look away from during our ordinary moments of existence. It enables us to confront the sources of our good and evil, our shortcomings and our strengths, our failures and our triumphs. It enables us to look at the nature of life so that we are captured neither by overbearing pessimism nor by naive optimism. It allows us a view of a world in need of redemption and of a life in need of full living.

The problem is that the ordinary rush of events makes the rationalization of our existence and the misinterpretation of our motives and activities an easy thing. We need meditation—some time in each day, if possible—even if we can't get to a desert place, in which to let life come to us truthfully and simply. Meditation turns us toward what is happening so that we can understand it; it does not direct us to a world outside ourselves in which we may seek some kind of refuge.

And contemplation relates us to truth. It may not always relate us to **the truth** that is promised in so many forms of meditation. We may not arrive all at once—indeed, some of us may never arrive—at the center of our being, but real meditation allows us to get closer to simple truths about ourselves that have to be faced. We get at **the truth** by moving closer to small truths. This is a difficult business, but it is essential for a mature life.

Human beings are not called to float away on a cloud of unknowing, chanting their mantra while reality drifts further out of their reach. We must be as wary of mass-produced meditation as we are of mass-produced dreams, as careful about believing their promises as we would those of a politician bent on election. The world is there and meditation opens us to it. It never, in any circumstances, is meant to close us off from it.

The way we were

Perspective is a hot topic of conversation in the modern-day world. We are always trying to correct somebody else's perspective or perhaps discover our own on certain questions. We can hardly escape time, that mysterious substance in which we are so firmly anchored, but we like to shift our feet and peer now this way, and now that, in order to see things from different angles. We like to look around while we are making the trip.

Time is one of our major mysteries, of course; our sense of time and the way it passes is a major life experience that seems subtly altered by various emotional and physical states. We know that the time sense is changed, for example, by taking certain drugs. So, too, it has been suggested, it was the time sense that was somehow slightly altered for the men who worked in the dead emptiness on the moon's surface. Of all their measured reactions, their sense of time was most keenly affected! The way we view time, we will one day more wisely understand, tells us a great deal about ourselves.

Some of us value time very highly. There are other cultures that don't esteem it quite the same way. In some lands the people are far more approximate in their attitude toward the clock, and their lives seem more spacious and unhurried because of this outlook. Americans are always rushing to meet deadlines, glancing at the clock and back to their work, even their play, with a steady and familiar anxiety.

Some of us describe ourselves best in temporal terms. We say that we are always right up to date on certain things. Others of us may say that we are always running behind. Some people are terribly uncomfortable unless they can get everything done well ahead of time. But what exactly does it mean to be on time anyway? Who sets the clocks, and what is proved by some of our more obsessive styles of dealing with time's passage?

In our own time

It may be a different thing to be a person of one's own time. We would all like to think of ourselves this way, but we recognize that there are people who live as though time had stopped. They are, we say informally, people who seem to come from another age. It may be because of their values or their outlook or the way they dress or wear their hair. Whatever it is, they project a sense of time long gone and nurtured, like nearly extinct plants, in their private gardens.

Being people of our own time means that we are aware of our world and of each other, that we have a sense of the meaning of things and that we do not hold back from entering into our share of existence. We need a clear perspective on where we fit into and how we regard time. As we course through the stages of growth plotted by psychoanalyst Erik Erikson, we all must finally come to a point where our concern is with people who belong to the future. *Generativity* is the name given to a whole bundle of attitudes that say that we are more concerned about those who will live after us than we are just about ourselves. We all get to the point where our growth depends on our capacity to look forward with real concern.

Where do we fit in?

If we take the time to explore our own perspective, where do we fit in to the flow of history? How do we look on ourselves? In which direction are we facing, backward or forward? Is there really leisure to moon over or mourn the way we were? The question comes down to asking ourselves whether we are living for yesterday or for tomorrow. There are many implications to whichever answer we give.

Living for yesterday suggests that we may spend most of our time remembering, straining to see backward into the mist of times that are forever gone. It is true that we usually only remember the good things of our lives clearly, but we run the danger, if we look only backward, of being too concerned with the bad things that have happened to us. We may, for example, sharpen the axes of revenge, grinding away in our backward perspective with such intensity that we grind down our teeth and wear ulcers into our stomach linings in the process.

Nostalgia may be fun, but living in the glow of shallow reminiscences, testing our intellects only on trivia, is bound in the long run to prove disappointing and undernourishing. It isn't very healthy to think that the only good things that have ever happened occurred a generation ago. Yet many of us think that the best of times are long gone, that things can never be put right again. That is the perspective of pessimism.

Looking only at what has taken place already may focus us too much on our own faults or shortcomings. We can take too much account of what has held us back, for example, of some handicap that we have allowed to dominate us too long, or some failure that we have allowed to haunt us too much.

When we live too much in past memories of what we have done wrong, we feed ourselves on guilt. This doesn't make a very tasty meal, but some people can't break the habit of ordering it. They are trapped in their own guilt, and they go on punishing themselves for things they should bury with other past events. When we are too mesmerized by guilt, we refuse to live in the present and we can hardly glance at the future. We then find it hard to believe in forgiveness, second tries, or even our own better possibilities. Guilt makes victims of people who can only remember what they did wrong. It is even worse when we only remember and count up what those around us have done wrong.

The trouble with living in the past is that it is really an elaborate fiction. We are not really there. We are in the present, like it or not, and we miss it completely because of our preoccupation with our previous history. But it is only yesterday in our heads and in our hearts. All around us it is today. We have to get a foothold back in the present in order to begin to live with concern for those who come after us, with a lively commitment of what energies we still have to direct toward the future of our human family.

Life is not a disease

Unfortunately, in the rush of modern times many people believe that life is indeed a disease, an illness for which, at all costs, we must find the cure. These persons attempt to solve difficulties about living that are in fact totally unsolvable. It is as if they considered breathing a problem and somehow there must be a way of modifying or learning to do without inhaling altogether. Trying to solve the problem of being human is like trying to get rid of rainy days, wintertime, or loneliness.

We all suffer, if one cares to say it, from terminal humanity. There is no way to treat it, much less cure it. We learn to live with it by living life with as much of ourselves as possible. We are then immediately more at ease. And those other feelings— vague fears, uneasy expectations, feeling out of it—lessen in that instant.

This is not to say that we are thereby freed to lead slovenly or impulsive lives. Rather, we are more comfortable in living when we can stop arguing with our basic human condition. When we do what we can, offering our best disciplined performance in life, our peace comes from having a sense of self and a sense of purpose. Being human is not really the problem. We commit ourselves to a less than perfect humanity and discover the relief —faster by far than that promised in the painkiller ads on television—that this remedy brings.

People in the sun

You know that the season is changing as soon as people start sitting in the sun, turning slowly, almost like flowers, to follow its arc of flooding warmth. It is not just when young people start going to the beach to work on their suntans. And it is something that gets underway, even in northern climes, long before summer arrives. It is a human instinct if ever there was one, a sign of something we all have in common, one of those family traits that keeps showing up to remind us that we are all related to one another. Turning toward the sun is a simple strategy for all age groups, for older people on park benches and younger ones on rooftops, for the rich in their villas and the poor in their everyday surroundings.

The sun is the same for everyone, promise and fulfillment all at once, a hint about our bodies and their needs and a signal about our souls and their longings, the great free-flowing bath of warmth that loosens our bones and alerts us to better days. Sunshine is filled with vitamins, they say, but it is filled with hope too. And there is something vulnerable about human beings stretched out under the sun, whether they are buttered and lined up like buns in a bakery tray or whether they are sitting in an old chair in a quiet backyard. They are looking for warmth and healing, for the simple gifts that cost little but count for much. There is something to be learned about the human family as we watch it, in all shapes and sizes, lying beneath God's sun. There is something tender in the scene that displays so much of our homeliness and true beauty at the same time. It is hard to look at people, no matter what their other struggles or problems, as they lie in the sun and not feel more kindly toward them and everyone else who shares the human condition.

Waiting too

There is also wisdom and a real asceticism in learning how to wait. There are many occasions when we must allow time itself to have its way with us. These may be frustrating moments, especially if we are unwilling to delay our own gratification even for an instant. It is difficult in an environment that urges people to grab instantly at what they can enjoy even to care about the lessons of waiting. Waiting will, however, purchase for us the space in which we can possess our souls. And life is filled with waiting; we may do more of that than almost anything else. It is never without meaning because it allows us to do battle with the selfishness that closes us off from the concerns and rights of other persons. Learning to wait is learning to live in time and with other persons. When we can do this, we have sealed a treaty of peace with life itself.

Things that take time

Becoming our true selves: We do not achieve our identity overnight any more than we can snatch it from other persons and use it as if it were our own. Finding the truth about ourselves does not mean the immediate and impatient statement of all our saving feelings or discontents. It demands the kind of waiting of which we have just spoken, as well as a refined patience that understands how the control of our impulses is indispensable to our maturity as persons. We need the spaciousness of time in order to find out who we are and to put away the fears that make us look away from this or become dissatisfied with the reality of ourselves. Instant selfhood is almost always a counterfeit. There are those who promise it through books, fads, weekend therapy, and even prayer sessions. But it never comes that way. The true self waits for us in time and demands that we acknowledge and accept this as a condition for finding it.

Caring and mourning: Care that gives life to others is killed when we do not take time for it. It cannot be communicated outside the dimension of time. Caring is one of the treasures we must spend freely if we are to contribute to the healing process in those who have been variously wounded by life. Care must be present in friendship and love, the care that cannot be taken for granted or merely periodically reestablished by a bunch of flowers or a birthday card. Care takes some time every day and, as those who work in hospitals understand, it is not just a dutiful seeing to it that food and heat and medicine are provided on a regular basis. The heart of caring is communicated between persons who can still touch those who suffer with the genuine concern of their own personality. It is a common excuse to say that we are in too much of a hurry to care; that, however, is what kills care and, in the long run, kills people as well. The failure to take time to care not only kills those who are the object of our care; it also kills us because it means that something has frozen inside our souls.

Mourning is a common human experience, one that we avoid speaking about and one we would like to postpone or dull our senses to if it comes into our own lives. We would like to get it over and done with, and so our society has done away with the symbols of mourning that, in previous years, acknowledged the fact that it takes time to mourn our losses. Unless we are willing to spend time we cannot finish our mourning and we remain incomplete and nonintegrated in the efforts we make to live the rest of our lives. Mourning can only take place in and through time. Mourning is but one of the difficult experiences of life; other hurts need time to be understood and healed. But as a wise man once wrote, "Tis an ill cure for life's worst ills to have no time to feel them."

Being a friend or falling in love: It may seem, looking back, that becoming a friend or falling in love takes place in an instant. If we examine the experience, however, we discover that a long preparation through time precedes those moments in which friends finally recognize and respond to each other. If we do not surrender to time, we may never recognize our true selves or the true selves of others; we may not be able to enter those instants in which we see someone else in a way that no one else has ever seen him or her before. The magic may seem to come in a moment, but the learning that goes into real love begins long before lovers meet. Friends move toward each other through time. When they meet they are able to respond to all that they have come to recognize as valuable. Time is the tide that brings us together when we are ready for the challenge of friendship and love. There is nothing sadder than people who try to skip time in their pursuit of friendship and love. They want the goal of intimacy with other persons but they are unwilling to take the time for the inner growth that is the best guarantee that genuine intimacy will be achieved. Time may change lovers once they have met, but it is only through surrendering to its special discipline that they are prepared to find each other.

In-between times

These represent the no-man's-land of life, a place we have all visited but no one has successfully charted. We find ourselves there, like it or not, sometimes when it is the very last place we want to be. In-between times abound in everybody's life. They come in different shapes and under different headings, but the essential dynamic is similar in all of them.

In-between time is that space between the preparation and the event, between the over-and-done-with and the not-yet, the place we stand after we have given of ourselves but when we are not sure just how it is going to be received. It is something like waiting for your report card. Sometimes it is closer to waiting for the jury to come back or for your loan to be approved or for your X rays to be examined by the doctor. Writers live in it when they are waiting for the critics' reviews. There are elements of testing involved in it, but there is never any completely final exam. We just keep getting tested over and over again in a wide variety of ways throughout our lives.

This is not an experience to be ignored or overcome, not one to be branded as evil although it has elements of discomfort and tension. In-between times do offer us an occasion to learn more about ourselves and to deepen our grasp on our identity and on the meaning of our lives.

We can discover in an in-between time just how much our self-esteem may be involved in a certain situation. We find out something about the vulnerability of the fragile membrane that holds our egos together. We may be surprised to discover this side of ourselves, something we may perhaps look away from in more ordinary times. In-between times may also be threatening to us. We can use them, then, to reexamine ourselves and to get closer to the truth of our own existence.

There is no doubt that we can pretend that an in-between time does not really affect us. We can whistle through the dark or play it cool, consciously distracting ourselves but neither interrupting nor delaying the unconscious processes that are at work within us. We make ourselves more vulnerable by failing to acknowledge the possibility of our own disappointment. We complicate our lives by trying to shield ourselves from living in the midst of the crowding, hard truths of our existence.

In-between times offer us an opportunity to make an act of faith in ourselves. This is not an exaggerated commitment to pride but a willingness to have confidence in our abilities, even when the outcome of what we are involved in may cause us to modify our estimate of them.

It is not easy to live with hard knocks and disappointment, but if we can hold on to a sense of ourselves, building on the fact that we have done our best with as much integrity as possible, we can emerge with a deepened sense of ourselves. In-between times and their tensions allow us to gather ourselves together so that we can face the emerging truth more honestly. We have to look it straight in the eye so that we can live with an integrated sense of ourselves. Believing in ourselves in these moments does help to make us whole, perhaps on a smaller scale than we would have liked, but whole nonetheless.

This is as true when the outcome is likely to be good news as when it is likely to be bad. We must, after all, learn to handle our success as well as our failure. Sometimes we are more ready to admit failure than to own the legitimate successes of our human experience. We are not whole unless we learn to live with the truth about our talents. Otherwise we are like the person in the Gospel who buried the talents in the ground, desperately afraid to find out what could be done with them.

An in-between time makes us sure of one thing. When it is over we will be different, one way or another. And the direction and the meaning of the change are uncontrollable only if we ignore ourselves or shrug off the experience or fail to take it as a time to learn the lessons of life.

Life is filled with such gaps. Sometimes it seems that there are more gaps in life than closed places. We are always living in the gaps, in the spaces in between, in the hard-to-track open areas where everything that is important happens to us. One gap closes and another one opens with a subtlety of timing that is mysterious. Life is like a vast, shifting field, rippled now this way and now that by the wind. Something is always opening as something else closes, and it is our willingness to inhabit the gaps of our existence that enables us fully to come to terms with the meaning of our lives. We can look elsewhere but we will never find ourselves more truth than in the in-between times.

Our finest hour

We know what Churchill meant when he used the phrase about the flyers who won the Battle of Britain, but what do we—what does anybody—mean when we speak of a "finest hour"? There are variants to this. We sometimes look back, sighing a bit wistfully, to say of some occasion or endeavor that we were "at our best." It is easy enough to know what we are describing when we admit to being "at our worst," but what is the measure of our superlative efforts?

Sometimes we mean that we made the perfect rejoinder instead of thinking of it ten minutes later or the next morning. Our best in this situation is equated with our quickest, with a triumph rather than a setback, a win instead of a loss. And at other times we have a sense that something we did—teaching a class, giving a talk, doing a difficult job—demanded and got the best we could give of our wit and energy. And there are times when we are describing ourselves at our noblest and most generous, an occasion we would like to get into the permanent record when we wrestled selfishness at least to a draw in the struggle of life.

It is not something to worry about. For most of us, such occasions are not matters of hours but of minutes or split seconds—even instants—when we get it all together and touch the top of our human form. In fact, most of us live, if anywhere, in the comparative rather than the superlative degree. We are caught in the effort to do better and to be better, to give something more the next time even though it may be far from our finest or our best. Most human beings are aware of their shortcomings, of the liabilities that hang on their souls like liens on an unfinished house, and the overidealization of their possibilities is not something to tempt them. Getting through the day, or the next hour, giving what we can all the while—life is made up of these small increments of grace, each one a blessing for ourselves and others. This is the way of the human involvement in growth, and there is not much time for basking in the warm glow of recollection about our finest hours. We do well to manage the next ten minutes.

Not that we do not have best moments. It is just that we are usually the last ones to notice them or make a note of them. That is because we are at our best—even at our holiest—when we forget ourselves and give the best we have for a cause or for people outside ourselves. Our best is usually the moment in which we give what we have to those who need it. We never remember the moments in which we have forgotten ourselves. For believers, these are *the* moments; if anyone writes them down or congratulates us is a matter of no concern.

Sometimes these moments occur when we are aware enough of others and their hurts or needs that we don't do or say anything. We just stick with them, leaving them enough room for their private thoughts and feelings and not pressuring them while we remain present to them. Yes, some of our finest moments (let us forget the hours) are forged in silence, in letting people be, in respecting them enough not to trample on their souls. Maybe a great deal of what finally counts goes on in silence and in the gifts we can give away when we hear the needs of others and forget our own.

CHAPTER 2

A time to be born . . .

Beginnings

It is impossible for us to speak only of endings. The closing of the year makes us more keenly aware of the subject but it awakens us to the year that is just starting, and beginnings are small miracles too. Life does not belong to the embalmers or to the people who design the closing titles for movies. There is simply no place where "The End" flashes across our living activity. Although it is a pleasant dream, we never get to sail into the sunset, serenely confident that our problems are all resolved. We can, however, learn to live happily ever after.

The secret lies partially in learning how to begin all over again almost all the time. You finish one big problem and then another promptly rolls into its place. There is hardly a moment between these occurrences in which to draw our breath. It is as if our challenges and problems were suited up and waiting for us like eager substitute football players who cannot wait to get into the game. Living happily ever after depends on understanding that and always being ready to start over. Living happily depends a great deal on being able to enter into the wonder of beginning. We are always beginning. It is the other half of the mystery we feel so deeply as we cross the icy bridge that leads from one year to another. We are always meeting, starting afresh, finding new chances as well as new challenges. . . .

Think of all the times we have had to start—or to start over—on important experiences in our lives. We may even think of the false starts we have made and what we have learned from them.

Then, too, there are the good starts. There is nothing more exciting than the first moments of a long-planned trip. They disappear even as we sense them, and sometimes the rest of the journey is never quite as exhilarating as the spirit and hope with which we begin it.

Think of the times we have had to shift our plans and start out in a new direction. People do this all the time in a world in which second careers are not uncommon and in which, indeed, retirement itself is a very special kind of beginning again for those who understand the later years as a new and significant part of life.

We can think of all the hard starts we have experienced. These include the things that have been difficult for us to do but that we committed ourselves to carrying out anyway. Sometimes this consists in facing a difficult truth with someone we love; sometimes it lies in confronting ourselves when we have let ourselves drift too far in life and have had to force ourselves back to our tasks. Most persons could make a long catalog of the things they dislike, are afraid of, or lack the courage for—and yet they continually enter into them and work their way through them.

Men and women can look back on their first date, the discovery of a first close friend, or their first falling in love. They were all beginnings, all points at which something came alive in them for the first time, something that could not be called back or ignored. These are the events in which we learn who we are and consolidate our identity.

We might think of all the starting again that each one of us has been through. Most people would like to set aside ever having to start again at anything, and yet this challenge continually makes itself felt. We have to move and make new friends, we have to take on a new job and prove ourselves yet again in a strange situation. There seems to be no end to the beginnings that are invitations to define ourselves more clearly in life.

Those who are beginning to feel old only need to reflect for a few moments on all the firsts they have already successfully faced and all the beginnings in life that are still before them. Life may just be more exciting than they think.

Good beginnings

Think, for example, of all the varieties of coming home. There is a large measure of wonder in returning to loved ones after a long or a short separation. Some of the same mystery accompanies getting back to work after a long vacation or returning to some task we had to interrupt for one reason or another. There is a special kind of beginning that is associated with any purposeful return. That is why people like to get back to their roots, back to their own beginnings. It deepens our sense of ourselves in a way that very few other experiences could.

Think of the healing that takes place when enemies—or just quarreling lovers—return to each other in reconciliation. They never go back to where they were before. They really cannot do that. Reconciliation does not mean going back to old boundary lines. This approach may work in geography but it does not work in matters of the spirit. We are changed through injury, and when we are reconciled we meet again but in a different way. This is why reconciliation means that we are starting all over again, with wounds that may be healed but still reveal scars. There is something powerful that takes place when people can come back together again after traveling far away from each other.

People do not heal each other, you see, by good wishes, not even by prayers or imposing their hands on them. These are meant to be powerful and accurate symbols of the invisible transactions that accompany all real healing. But the symbols are empty unless we are there, making ourselves vulnerable once again, in an effort to face the wound honestly and either to seek or to give forgiveness. It is a beginning with profound implications.

Always there

Beginnings are available to us all the time. All that they require is that we be willing to see things freshly. Boredom may come more to persons who can look at the world from only one angle. In almost any line of activity repetition does not necessarily dull our sense of appreciation. The secret lies in shifting our position. The more we go over something—the more we read a poem or listen to a symphony—the more we may be able to see and hear hidden things. It is no surprise, for example, when people who are quite expert in one field or another say about something they work with all the time, "This is the first time I really understood it in this way." Their attitude is one of openness even to familiar territory where there is still always something to see.

We can do this in every season. Not one of them changes exactly like any other in all history. What is there for us to wait for? It works the same way with people. We have to shift our position for a moment in order to see them in a new light. Sometimes we can even see new sides to ourselves that we have not permitted ourselves to look at before. That means that we can always participate in a beginning, that we can always have the freshness of discovery, that we are never worn out and that the world around us is never used up by any of us.

What happens when we begin?

There is an undeniable excitement about any beginning. That is so because it requires us to draw the aspects of ourselves together. We cannot make any true beginning in a careless or distracted fashion. If we are not in it then there is no real beginning. One of the most important features of starting fresh on anything depends on our willingness to make ourselves more alive so that we can commit more of our truth and our energies to the situation.

This involves our quality of presence. How much of us is there and available to us for the effort? What special aspect of incarnation is involved in concentrating our strengths and attention on the task or the invitation to relationship that lies before us?

In other words, you have to be there in order to begin anything well. That is the essential ingredient in a good start for almost anything. That is what makes it a miracle. We come more to life and we sense our own identities more clearly at the sharply defined moments of starting on some activity. We can therefore share more of who we are with other persons.

Presence is at the heart of this small miracle of beginning. Relationships only grow dull when people fail to realize that they are always beginning afresh with each other, that they are involved continually in each other's possibilities. So beginning, and the special presence it demands of us, is essential to many of the things we long for—to friendship and love and forgiveness. One of the marvelous things we learn in the Scriptures is that God always makes room for us to begin again. There is no restriction to this on his part. It all depends on whether we are prepared to face our truth—good or bad—and head back into life in his presence.

Good to go away

This is what makes a homecoming, at the end of the day or at the end of a long journey, such a remarkable experience. It may be one of the most common that we have, and yet it never loses its wonder for those who know that it is more than just an occasion for casual greetings. Every time people who love each other come home again, they have a chance to come more alive in each other's presence. They live in the excitement of the beginnings that enable them to see each other freshly. When we are truly present to each other, no day can ever seem exactly the same as any other one.

Who do you think you are?

Here is one of our most common questions, one that is asked almost every day and usually in the context of mild indignation.

It's the kind of thing people say to someone who has over-stepped reasonable claims for attention or presumed too much in a certain situation. But it can also be asked in a calmer tone and with a different set of inflections. It would then reflect our concern about personal identity that has been almost a favorite plague of Americans for the last several decades.

Some people really haven't thought too much about it. They have accepted an identity given to them by other persons. They have hardly had room for a breath on their own, because some-one else has provided them with a role they are to play in life. There are expectations made, and sometimes it is easier to try to meet them than it is to find out why we are in conflict about them. When people get themselves into a role that does not match them, they sometimes discover that they can no longer find the room to turn around and make their way out. They have obligations that cannot be dismissed, or they feel they have gone too far or that they are unable to find their way back to the place where they belong.

This is a difficult situation, and it may be quite understand-able that such persons do not probe their psyches too deeply. They have to live as best they can in some kind of psychological compromise; such an adaptation is not ideal, but neither is it uncommon. Such persons need support and understanding and all the help we can give them so they can find satisfactions in extra work or hobbies that match their true identity. And some might just change and head in the direction they have always belonged if they feel there are friends who will stand by and understand them when they make such a bold move.

Of course, some people are very self-conscious. They are al-ways thinking about who they are and they want other people to think about it too. They are not so much conscious of others' expectations as they are of the impression they create. Their whole life is a work of art at which they diligently labor, knit-ting with the energy of Madame Defarge into the fabric of their days all the names and dates they hope will impress others with their importance. But self-consciousness has never been an at-tractive characteristic. It shows the world around us that we are not quite sure of who we are. It is a heavy weight that can drag people blindly to the ground.

Others purposely do not inquire about their identity because they are not very comfortable with themselves to begin with and not very confident in their own capacity to deal effectively with life. They spend their time trying not to think about themselves at all or trying to hide themselves from others. They stand back at the edge of the crowd or on the borderline of life like ungainly sophomores at the edge of the dance floor. They are victims of a different kind of self-consciousness, a stifling and smothering experience that is like a blight on their personalities. Awareness of the self is painful, and in trying to avoid it, they end up avoiding those circumstances that would bring them in close contact with others. In the long run they need the kind of liberation that only close contact with other persons can give them. Perhaps it is our task at times to help such persons be more self-confident and more at ease because we understand and make room for them in our lives without embarrassing them.

There are many other categories of identity that we might explore. We may fit into them ourselves at times. There is, for example, the strange "great sinner syndrome" that occurs to people whenever they think about themselves. Who do they think they are? They think they are the world's greatest transgressor, headed straight for the *Guinness Book of Records* for their inner depravity. This is not likely, of course, because, hidden as the name of the world's greatest saint is, so too is that of the world's greatest sinner. Few of us are bold enough to be great sinners anyway. There is something sad about this, because it suggests that few of us are passionate enough to be great lovers either.

Closely allied are those people who think they are the only ones who have ever had such problems, whatever those problems might be. This is highly unlikely as well. People only think this way until they read Ann Landers's newspaper column to find how varied human experience really is. We are already better off when we realize that we are not the only ones who have ever had problems. There is support in realizing that we are only sharers in a deep and complex condition that is never problem free.

Then there are the favorite identities of the fearful, the people who try to make it through life by taking over somebody else's identity. These people might well fit into what radio humorists Bob and Ray call their "Person of the Month Club." "Once you're enrolled," they promise, "the postman will bring to your door every thirty days all the documents you need to assume a new and fascinating identity." The comedians claim to have testimonials in this regard; a gentleman from Ohio writes: "For years I have wanted to shun my old identity and become the Shah of Iran." And an Arizona lady rhapsodizes: "Imagine a simple housewife like me becoming Vaughan Monroe." A woman from Oregon claims that "life has taken on new meaning for me since I became Gladys Knight and the Pips. I can never thank you enough." A good laugh is probably the best way to deal with the minor presumptions that go into affecting the mannerisms, the dress, or the hairstyles of the great and mighty ones around us. It isn't that we take away their strength by imitating them; it is that we never discover all that we can possess ourselves.

Yes, a sense of humor helps, especially at those moments when we have wandered far from our true possibilities. There is nothing like a good laugh to get us back on the right track. After all, we are part of a big family in which very little that happens to us is really new as far as the experience of human history is concerned.

Perhaps it would be most selfish if, in defining our identity, we thought we were the only persons who ever knew true love, for this is highly unlikely, too. True love comes in many forms, and it generally arrives unexpectedly. It is found in places where people don't look for it and it comes inevitably into the lives of people who have achieved some comfort with their identity and who are no longer seeking to impress others or make sure that their appearance will make them the center of attention wherever they go. They are interested, rather, in the substance of life.

True love finds its way into the lives of people who are unselfconscious in a healthy way. There is room enough in their

life space then for another to enter. They can see the other as
separate and deserving of a response. This is how love begins
wherever it is true. If we stop being so concerned about ourselves we will be able to recognize that love is not an exclusive
or rare thing. It is reassuring to realize that like the Asian flu,
there is a lot of it going around.

Pictures of ourselves

Self-knowledge. Or course, but, as St. Augustine said of reform,
not yet. This is the way many of us feel about learning more
about ourselves. We honestly do want to understand ourselves
more; why do we hesitate? Perhaps because what we sometimes
learn can be discouraging, and if we've already had enough bad
news in a day the last thing we want is somebody else telling us
off or some new evidence of our shortcomings. Further data
about our imperfection are particularly discouraging as the year
or the day comes to a close.

Nobody ever seems shy about telling us what is wrong with
us anyway. That brand of self-knowledge seems to be in great
supply. But, as you may have noticed, we seldom change just
because other people tell us that we should. Most of the things
that people point out about our failings are already well known
to us, and it is less than encouraging, especially when we are
trying to do our best, to have them recounted once more.

There are gentler ways of discovering truths about ourselves.
These opening doors welcome us into the human situation
without forcing us to walk through a harsh gauntlet toward
wisdom. One of the best ways of discovering something about
our identity is through recognizing what we hold in common
with everybody else. There are certain very human things that
we all do—like touching wet paint despite the warning signs—
that reveal us as more alike than different, more like possible
brothers and sisters than strangers. We say, when we see these
things, "How human!" We are willing to forgive people even of
the worst sins of pompousness and pretense when something
human shows through at the same time. As long as they have a

human side, we can find good reason to keep up our relationships with them.

In observing these foibles we are really hearing the faint echoes of very important aspects of our human history. These common activities contain hints, for example, about our extraordinary curiosity, about our basic simplicity, and about our sometimes misplaced self-consciousness. They tell us something of that mysterious quality known as charm. There may be signals, too, of more primitive aspects of ourselves, symbols of activities that men and women have been doing in the same way, in a fashion appropriate to their historical period, for hundreds of years. We can look back across the ages and see the cave man and woman as very different from us and yet strangely like us at the same time. Call these things oddities, if you wish, but they are really more similar to a likeness running through our whole family album. What are some of these things? They include:

Looking for change in pay telephones after we have hung up. One of the most universally observable phenomena is the search for stray coins that goes on in telephone booths across the world; it is a trait that does not depend on the age, sex, or affluence of the caller. Distinguished men in Homburg hats as well as children barely big enough to reach the phone manifest the same instinct. Some people learn to search in a more sophisticated manner, of course, as though they were genuinely searching for a coin returned after a busy signal. Others learn how to mask the move of their inquisitive fingers by looking the other way with the marvelous innocence of a confidence man picking a pocket. Still others go at it more aggressively, as though they feel that everybody recognizes the right of the public to take what they can from the utilities that, as they see it, take as much as possible from them.

Maybe it tells us something about our animal beginnings, but *most people like to pick at things.* They pick at taped-down edges on almost everything; they even pick at themselves. Very few people have not had the following sentence addressed to them several times during their lives: "Stop picking at that!" This instruction doesn't stop us, however, and whether it is a sign of something primitive about us or of something profoundly inquisitive about us, it is something that all persons can recognize as typically human behavior.

There are many variations on this third common activity, but one example will do. *It is not unusual for persons to use the backside of fresh guest towels so the towels appear never to have been used at all.* There is something strange in this behavior, but it is not very rare. Perhaps it is a particular affliction of obsessives who hate to see order violated and who like to retain at least the superficial semblance of neatness in their lives. One must ask if this behavior is not second cousin to sweeping things under rugs or learning to mask our writing when we are unsure of whether the letter should be *i* or *e* by working it into what looks like an almost natural blot.

There are a number of similar shortcuts that even the most perfectionistic can engage in at times; we should not be surprised at finding examples of these things in our own lives. We should be more comforted than disturbed at finding so many small signs of our common human heritage.

Make your own list

It is a good idea to make a list of your own foibles. These usually outnumber major faults, and there is something mildly charming if not totally attractive about them. You have to smile as you make such a list because you can recognize yourself in these behaviors that link us together in such a simple way. Such behaviors help us to identify ourselves as members of the same family. As small as they are, they are big enough to illumine our similarities in moments when we may be preoccupied with our differences. They are signs of our frailty and our need for each other. Who could forgive us for these but someone who understands them? As long as we can smile at these activities, we can have compassion for each other.

Are you more interesting than you think?

Probably so, even though many persons say that nothing much happens in their lives, or that they are easily bored in an existence that is as dull as last year's fallen leaves. Actually we are all far more intriguing than we think. Spring and Easter provide a good time to think about it. If we listen carefully we can hear the rise and fall of a hundred inner tides. If we look we may be able to see the surprises that fall like August stars across our awareness every day.

The contemporary prophets of a new consciousness want to awaken people to an absolute kind of fulfillment, a revived perfectionism that will allow them to fly high above the human situation. And such stress is involved in all the currently advocated breakthroughs: We speak here of something simpler, truer, and always at hand, something to make us friendlier with ourselves, and something that allows us to perceive our ordinary wonders instead of urging us to strain after extraordinary ones.

The trouble is that we don't look or listen acceptantly enough; we are half ashamed of the odd pieces of our humanity and, far from understanding them, we sneak through the back alleys of life carrying them awkwardly in our arms, like a bundle of contraband literature. We are tempted to breakthroughs in consciousness to escape from the dead ends, the dullness, the stacked-up shortcomings of life. And all the while fascinating things are occurring inside us that give testimony to the varied but unique qualities of our own personalities.

Take, for example, *the crazy things we do.* And we do them all the time; it is just that most of the time we don't let ourselves notice. We begin, of course, by realizing that because we do crazy things on a fairly regular basis does not mean that we are going crazy ourselves. It just means that healthy and quite normal people are capable of behaving in highly unusual ways, that there is some "crazy part" in all of us that reasserts itself and rejects taming or logical explanation. It doesn't help to get mad at ourselves about such a situation; it helps enormously to be able to recognize and thereby feel less estranged from what seem to be alien sources of our behavior.

It also helps to know that everybody is like this, that our temporary craziness is a sign of our relatedness, a reassurance rather than a rejection of our normalcy. This is why we may find ourselves taking unnecessary chances while driving or just making our way across the street. As a matter of fact, people tell us about these moments all the time; they say, "I just did something crazy," or "I'm a little crazy today."

We may, in fact, hear ourselves saying these things once in a while. Pay attention! This shows that we can all live with a measure of contained erraticism and that we should not be too alarmed about it. The thing to do when we realize that we have been swinging from our own deep end is to acknowledge it. It helps to be able to say, "That's just the crazy part of me," because it puts it in perspective. We know that it is not the whole of us and, with a philosophical—perhaps an almost winking—acceptance of our occasional oddities, we will sleep more comfortably.

Then, too, we could all make a long list of *the neurotic things we do,* a bill of particulars about the defensive adjustments we use at least in minor ways in otherwise quite normal lives. Watching ourselves, we might observe that whenever we have a minor setback, even an imagined one, we may handle it by an automatic indulgence of ourselves. If we have even a small loss, we feel entitled to gratification almost on the spot. It is a common pattern, and as long as it does not become a way of life, there is not much harm done. Sometimes it is a necessity and sometimes it works fairly well. Haven't you ever gone out and bought something after a disappointment and felt better for it? That beats self-pity, sulking, or even plotting revenge.

The thing people frequently forget about the neurotic solutions they occasionally produce is that they work—maybe not as well as a mature acceptance of life's unevenness, but the best of us is not always perfectly mature. So when we spoil ourselves a little it is not as tragic as spoiling ourselves a lot. It helps us cope until we can react more maturely, and that is not all bad. That's what people have to get by on at times.

Neurotic evidence abounds in the daily life of good people. Most of us exaggerate a little, are known to tell little white lies from time to time, and can cite multiple examples of inconsistencies in our attitudes and behavior. We need the viewpoint that recognizes this as the neurotic parts of ourselves, allows us to laugh or at least smile at ourselves, and pull ourselves together again.

There are numerous examples of *psychopathic things* that we all do or at least savor from time to time. We can all give in unexpectedly to impulse, we can con others in small ways, and we may even be inclined to take small things to which we have no title—echoes, all of these, of mildly psychopathic or antisocial inclinations. Perhaps we sense them better when we find ourselves identifying with the lawbreaker, especially if he is a colorful character. So we root for the bank robbers to escape the police dragnet or hope for the acquittal of the charming embezzler whose audacious acts against society give us some real vicarious satisfaction. Recognizing these hints of the rogue in ourselves should not destroy us, either; we have to learn to live with the little psychopath within, knowing that this is only a small part—an interesting part—of what we are.

More serious, however, is the discovery of the mean part of the self: the evener of scores, the hard-hearted and selfish part of the ego that can hurt other people without seeming to try. How often this part of the self gets the upper hand merely because we do not keep it in perspective or fail to acknowledge the fouled emotions on which it feeds and grows strong. The mean part of ourselves gets out when we deny or attempt to disguise our real feelings. That is when things back up, like clogged pipes, and our calm is betrayed by the emotions we have not faced honestly.

We are redeemed—resurrected, indeed—by other discoveries about our possibilities. There is far more to us than we may at first suppose, and it is all interesting. And if we can acknowledge our occasional capacity for neurosis and meanness, we should also be able to admit our capacity for goodness and nobleness. We may look away from our goodness—a gift for tenderness, say—and try to act tough. But we are intrinsically more interesting than the stereotype of the unfeeling American. Human beings are filled with poetry, with the promise of love, with the strength of trust and belief and the powers of hope and healing.

This is what we are really like when we give ourselves a chance and enough room to share our unique selves with the world. We are interesting because in our unaffected human presence we have the ingredients for the good life; the power, in fact, to give and expand the lives of our family, our friends, our people, or our students. A great wonder, this core of our own humanity, and it is stronger than our sometimes craziness, our periodic neurosis, and far more refreshing than our meanness is depressing.

We begin to appreciate the organic religiosity of life when we see how filled with small deaths is the long sweep of our days. There is a death to undergo in facing everything that is real about us, in admitting and living with the frustrating shortcomings of our craziness and our meanness. But that is also the way toward what is luminous and joyful, the multiplied mystery of the resurrections we experience when we are simply honest and true with ourselves and others. We may once have been filled with darkness but now we are filled with light—and the occasional shadows and temporary eclipses certify that the drama of salvation is repeated daily in ordinary lives such as our own.

How do people describe their lives?

There is something profoundly touching—and powerfully resurrecting—in listening to people tell us about their lives. Pause and listen and you will also be filled with wonder at the way in which good persons, even after long and painful journeys through existence, make themselves whole as they make peace with themselves. "Well," the old lady says from her nursing home bed, "I'm pretty good. I have lots to be thankful for." Or the dying man with the bristling fringe of white hair who struggles for breath but says, "My life's been more good than bad at that . . ." Or take one not so old but a crippled and blind woman who, despite her troubles, says in a joyful voice, "I have had many happy days. . . ." "Well, it's not been so bad after all," another older person says. "Lots of tears but lots of laughter too. . . ."

Listen to those people; they are like wise and weatherbeaten farmers who know that the grain isn't all the same quality but who are grateful for the harvest anyway. They finger life, like the farmer does the grains of wheat, recognizing the chaff that is mixed inevitably with the simple solid kernels. They feel what is good and know that it will endure. There are few experiences more humbling than listening to the old and sick sift the harvest and pronounce that despite its mixed qualities, it is still good. This is the kind of peace that comes for those who learn to live the life that is possible, if imperfect, rather than perfect but finally impossible.

Where do we live?

Well, one says, that is an easy question if all that is required is an address; it gets a little more complicated if we try to chart our exact personal location, our current point of progress given the nature of the winds and the state of our energy supply. People, of course, are always asking us about where we are at and where we are coming from, questions that suggest bad grammar and an inexact sense of spiritual geography. Sighing to ourselves, we sometimes confess that we don't seem to be getting anywhere even though we are trying very hard. And at other times, emerging into the light from the murkiness of a down period, we are not even sure where we have been.

Yet the question is worth asking because it makes us think of the eddying mystery of time and place in which our perspective shifts and our exact location is often difficult to determine. Not for nothing is the colloquial phrase about people—*other* people, that is—that says they live in the past. And improvident people, sometimes charming despite their impulsiveness, are said to live for the moment. If we observe ourselves we sometimes discover that we range across the borders of time like scouting parties on an uneasy frontier. We may fancy ourselves as modern, but we may not be living in the present at all. Where, according to our deepest internal sense, do we spend the gift of life?

It is easy to be contemporary but it is difficult to be truly modern in a mature sense of the term. There is no fundamental difficulty in changing one's styles or one's furniture so that everything is in place before most people even realize that fashions have changed. It is far more challenging to be modern in a sensitive and totally human manner. Such an achievement rests on our capacity to hear and understand what novelist Anthony Powell has described as the "music of time." This is not the same as current events. It is connected not so much with the facts of history as with the truth about ourselves and our relationships with others. These are at the core of a life that has meaning, and they are not experiences that take care of themselves.

A husband and wife, for example, cannot live on remembered love alone. They cannot smile in recollection of the way things used to be and think that they can travel on this with much zest or satisfaction into the future. Living in the present requires not only listening to each other but a readiness to make regular adjustments as well. The strength of love depends not on grand gestures or large presents but on the steady, small moments of growth.

Growth sounds good but it is inherently disturbing; it depends on our living in the ever-processing present, with those we love or serve as they are now rather than the way we remember them or wish they were. Love stays alive not when people resign themselves to a stereotype of each other but when they are attuned and responsive to the changes—some from age, some from new experiences, some from uncharted depths—that take place in each other all the time. That is not an easy thing to do, but it is precisely the spiritual invitation that keeps us alive.

Life, of course, would be easier if we all stayed the same, but it would, in the long run, turn out to be dull, too. Is there anything more stolid than a person who never changes an opinion, never tries to understand anything, or never surprises us? Life consists in keeping up, not with the Joneses, but with each other.

Things that "almost happen"

There are territories large and small, dukedoms as well as king-
doms, in the universe of relative time. Think, for example, of
people who dwell near the edges of experiences that "almost
happen." Hawthorne wrote once of the "airy steps" of such
occurrences. They are not, however, ghosts, for they have a dis-
cernible mass and weight around which persons can organize
their lives. Such notions provide hints about the way some of us
order our perceptions of time and place and personality. As
such, these things that almost happen have a special power because they become the focal points for many of life's events.

Listen and you will hear people who speak mostly about
things that almost happen, of places they might have gone and
things they might have done, of great people they almost met or
great disasters to which they were almost witnesses. Is it just
wistfulness at the heart of this subjunctive mood? Are such
statements the flickers of regret at decisions not made and roads
not chosen? Or are they the rationalized explanations for a life
never quite fully lived, of personalities still in need of transfu-
sions from the realm of possibilities to bolster their sense of
reality? There is a wide variety in this vicarious imagining.
Sometimes it is sad, as when some persons go through life re-
peating endlessly how they might have been here or there—
next to greatness or splendid opportunity all the time—if only
they had had a break, or things had been different.

Then there is the person who resents you because you *did*
what they only *thought of* doing. There is a wide variety of this
strange species of envy. "We were going to buy this house but
you made an offer first." "I would have given them a place to
stay but they were already settled in with you." The latter
phrase is particularly vexing because persons who make such
statements actually take a kind of credit for something they
didn't do.

Then there are those who look back at a life they might have
led but didn't. They manage, however, to convey their potential
greatness—no, their achieved greatness—as though they obvi-

ously have succeeded magnificently in a wholly imagined career. Thus the person who says, "I could have tried out for the Yankees" has the bearing of a man ready to accept nomination to the Baseball Hall of Fame.

What we need, common sense tells us, is the right perspective on ourselves, a less grandiose and more realistic appraisal of the space we actually do fill here and now. We need a look at what we are really like and how we deliver ourselves and our talents in our lives and relationships. Are we inhabiting the moments we have, or do we invest in times that are not yet or in events that never were? Are we committed to the plain truth of our lives, or are we caught up in the complicated distortions that make it difficult for us to grasp the meaning of life's more important times?

And with whom?

It is impossible to separate these questions, except in the contained passion of philosophers for distinctions, and this one is, after all, the most significant just as its answer is the most defining of our true selves. The inquiry proceeds into the heart and the mode of its sharing. We learn about ourselves and the tasks of life that lie still before us when we chart the measure of our presence to those around us. How much are we actually with those we claim to love, and how much do we allow them to be with us?

Perhaps nothing is more vital for our human and spiritual survival than letting ourselves out and letting others in. It is, in fact, that which delivers meaning, that deep sense that we have not missed life, that we have entered the temple of its mystery. Presence lets us feel the quiet peace of deep love and gives us a new sense of time; it is strength against a sometimes blind and hurting world and the place for the celebration of joy at wounds healed and difficult things worked through. It is the space for the magic of play, the unadorned wonder of doing nothing aimlessly and hilariously with someone else; it is the seal set on keeping faith with each other.

How anguishing to have good news and no one you really

want more than anything else to tell about it. How diminished the existence of a person who is armored against ever missing anyone else, secure against being missed as well. And who is it we would like to have near if we were ill or in trouble? Who rescues us from drowning in our own self-pity except those who stay with us in the darker moments of our struggle? Who is it, in other words, we count on for the validation of our lives; who, indeed, counts on us for the same free gift?

It takes time to locate the precious moments as well as the people with whom we lay hold of life. And it is easy to be so busy that we leave out what they need and what we need; it is not to be doing something or necessarily going somewhere. The secret lies in being with each other in the thousand ways that seem too small for naming yet constitute the very soul of the presence through which we feel the grace of life.

And in what way?

A modern examination of conscience insists that we get at the root of our moral style. This is revealed, of course, in the way we live with each other through all the ordinary moments of existence. Morality may be tested in dramatic, or seemingly dramatic, crises but it is built in the long growing season of everyday choices. And the mode of our self-revelation and engagement with others reveals our basic morality better than anything else.

Moral living has a shape, and it is one that is a profile of ourselves. The trouble with reserving discussions of morality for weighty events is that it gets things out of proportion; it makes us think that our redemption depends only on the big choices or those connected with certain subjects such as sex. So the wells are sunk in this field, pumping up gushers of guilt and distracting us from the full truth of our moral style, which is revealed in a hundred other ways.

Let us consider sex for a moment, though, with the hope that preachers and moralists can transfer some of their correct judgments about sex without love to other aspects of life. Sex-without-love is indeed a disordered human transaction, the use of another for selfish pleasure. But sex is not the only arena in which such transactions take place. And some of them are engineered by individuals who are self-consciously moral and religiously motivated in their own eyes. For example, the ecclesiastic who makes a fuss over rich parishioners, one eye already agleam in anticipation of the financial reward that may follow, goes through a transaction as loveless and crass as any we know.

So it struck me with the bright-eyed clergyman I met on a plane recently. He told me that he had been pleased with his trip; he had made a number of "good contacts." Translated, this means people who could be used in the future, persons responded to not for themselves but for their potential in delivering influence or money later on.

Well, we are all vulnerable here, there is no doubt of that, and perhaps we need a confrontation with our own dealings with others to see if they are more morally informed than the sex-without-love that is so easy to condemn.

Why so surprised?

A recent news story expressed at least mild surprise at the findings of Northwestern University archaeologists excavating an old Indian settlement in west central Illinois. "Contrary to popular conception," the author notes, these Indians "who lived . . . in 6500 B.C. were not primitive savages who struggled just to survive. They were a comparatively sophisticated people who ate well on the abundant wildlife around them, lived in families in substantial wooden huts, the earliest houses known in America, and did not fight with their neighbors."

The question is: why are we surprised to find that people who lived before us seem to be so much like us? Just a few years ago, for example, a group of anthropologists said that use of the term "primitive man" was inappropriate since the discovery of the elaborate religious systems ancient people had devised to explain the universe and guide their lives. Why be surprised that the Indians of the American Midwest showed no signs of violence, not even having fortifications around their homes? It is familiar but not amazing to learn that they had pet dogs and that they knew how to preserve and store food.

One of the great lessons of life, as psychiatrist Harry Stack Sullivan said, is that we are all "much more simply human than anything else." How many scenes of weeping widows and children from the Far, Middle, or Near East do we need in order to recognize each other as members of the same family? Perhaps we must make a pilgrimage back in time, back to the silent central Illinois Indian dig that now speaks so clearly to us about how remarkably alike all of us who share the gift of life really are.

We may be surprised but we should rather be comforted and strengthened by such discoveries. They are an invitation to compassion and understanding in a world where people are so afraid of their differences that they forget how much they are alike.

Just follow the directions . . .

Cracker boxes are a case in point. They are splendidly designed, colorfully printed, and they bristle with dotted lines and tabs to be reinserted to ensure freshness. There is an oddity here, however. The directions, printed in fairly basic English, frequently tell you how to close the top and, as smugly as a British ace climbing into his Sopwith Camel, say nothing about getting it open.

Most people use the tear-it-open-as-best-you-can method. This usually destroys the directions and the cardboard tabs of their concern. The cabinets of America are filled with cardboard boxes that prove the difficulty involved in giving and taking directions. And yet giving directions remains a favorite pastime of the self-consciously wise, just as trying to follow them remains the province of the determinedly good-natured and sincere.

There are instructions for just about everything, careful plans that cover everything from growing houseplants to making love, from learning how to pray to learning how to play the stockmarket. My guess is that attics, kitchen drawers, and glove compartments of America are filled with pamphlets, books, and handbills containing half-read sources and half-finished products attesting to instructions that have failed us.

There are many times in life—some of the most highly valued of our experiences among them—when trying to follow the instructions just doesn't work. There are many human enterprises, like making friends or being faithful, that we just have to get the hang of on our own. Nobody can teach us most of what is important in life. Some can make it easier for us to learn but, if they are wise, they will try to stay out of our way as we grope toward our goals.

We only tear at things when the instructions betray or frustrate us, as in the case of the cracker boxes. Left on our own, with people to love and care for us staying close to us, we can find the best way to do the really sacred things in life. And taking responsibility for finding our own way remains a good simple definition of the moral life.

CHAPTER 3

And a time to die . . .

Why do things have to end?

This is a question for the closing days of summer, which are charged with intimations of slowly collapsing vacations. Even the air hangs differently—as it does across the gaps of life—and we can feel the slowly convulsing shift of seasons in our bones. Why do things have to end? It is the question of the child who would defy his own sleepiness to play forever in the falling darkness. It is the question of lovers who would stop the earth's clocks to hold on to their best moments together. It is the question that people ask about the good times that took so long to come and such a short time to go, while the bad times never seem to end at all.

This remains one of the most poignant of all human questions, one that is bittersweet at best to people who have seen the sun go down on remembered days that have never come in quite the same way again. People often look back on their lives to some period that was difficult—a time when they had to work hard to make a success of themselves, their marriage, or their family—and recall it as the happiest of times. Why did these have to come to an end? People never stop shaking their heads about good times past. Proust made a career of it.

This is not very different from the feeling that the artist or the writer has; his or her greatest happiness is during the struggle to shape a private vision into words or to carve it into marble. Once this is ended, the creator never feels quite the same. He or she experiences what the philosopher Nietzsche called "the melancholy of everything completed."

The heightened moments when we rise above our ordinary experience are those we describe as times of ecstasy. It is impossible to recapture them and a consistent sadness of our human state that we must permit them to end. There is nothing more painful for us than intermission periods, those times between important events when we are left like travelers with our luggage packed and nothing to do but bear the long restlessness of waiting to go.

Whether it is as lovers or artists, we never get everything said in just the way we would like. We never quite find the right symbols or gestures to speak the truths of our overflowing hearts. Neither do we ever enter as deeply as we would like into all the best moments that we share with each other. The candle sputters out; the good wine is spent. The measure of our yearning is the measure of our dead-end limits in trying to accomplish all this. The fact that things come to an end merely confronts us with our longing, with our profound urge to shatter the barriers of our human state, as well as with our desire to challenge not only sundown but death itself. Facing the end of things opens us to a sense that we can only be fulfilled finally in God himself. All the tremors that we experience in our frustration about passing seasons and ending phases of our lives are hints of everything that lies yet before us. We find signals about our future in our feelings every day as the sun goes down a minute earlier and as we grow a little older and a little more eager to lay a firm hold on our lives.

What really ends?

The only things that do come to an end are those which are incapable of growth or development—in other words, those things that are untouched by life, things that are unloved. The terrible finality of death hangs over only those events in which we have refused to invest life itself. These are dead from the beginning, ended before they start because they are deprived of the spirit and spark of life. They include:

Relationships in which we have not really been present, where we have made a checkmark of sorts but withheld ourselves. We are often present bodily—as we are in crowds or at anonymous lunch counters—without having to give any of the substance of our spirit. It is easy to sit and look at another and not hear a thing he or she is saying, even when that person is a relative or a friend. This happens when we are so preoccupied with ourselves and our own cares that we literally cannot share any real life with the other person. It can happen in a thousand ways—in a classroom where a teacher does not care about his pupils or in an unloving sexual relationship where tenderness is as dead as a straw flower. All these things are lifeless before they begin; no artificial respiration can touch them, and they leave us with a sense of numb incompleteness.

The things that we kill and refuse to resurrect. This also has to do with personal relationships; here, however, we can observe a beginning but it is a promise of life that is not redeemed. Relationships, in other words, can be put to death—sometimes violently and sometimes through a long and agonizing illness. This happens when, for whatever reason, people stop working at deepening and extending the meaning of what they share with each other. Many husbands and wives start out being in love, only to discover that it becomes difficult after a while, that love does not take care of itself and that the challenge of change mounts too swiftly for them. This occurs in other friendships and in different situations. When things get complicated—when, in other words, the real tests of life come—some people will not pay the price; they prefer to let the relationship die rather than transform themselves in order to keep it alive. They breed a special kind of deadness and, as long as the price of revitalization seems too risky for them, they write endings that are quite final.

Perhaps the worst form of this is found in married people who do not realize that their love for each other is also bound to be marked with ends and beginnings. One of the saddest misinterpretations of love springs from the idea that it will always be the same, that it will constantly generate the same feelings and provide the same energies of sacrifice that it does at the beginning of the marriage. When people are unprepared for the fact that these first feelings end or, more accurately, are transformed through time, they are unprepared either to understand or to respond to the steady need to change which defines every kind of real love.

"Marriages may be made in heaven," Ann Landers once wrote, "but the maintenance work must be done on earth." This catches something that lovers must learn if they are to save their relationship from dying at their own hands. Even the deepest and most secure relationships of love are marked by development and constant change; this necessarily occurs because of new experience, new education, the coming of children, and the other many important events that form the context for any living relationship. Married people should be prepared not to hold on to a memory of what they used to feel toward each other but to look more deeply into the evolving experience they must continue to share with each other if they are not to put their love to death. Lovers must, in other words, infuse their relationship with an ever-expanding awareness of each other and a willingness to grow together to avoid the death-dealing blow of growing separately and in opposite directions from each other.

Love does not come to an end, as St. Paul tells us so beautifully, precisely because its nature demands a constant vital investment and reinvestment of the self. Love lives on the fresh energies we give it every day. This is why genuine love is never boring and why people who love each other can experience such steady joy in each other's presence. It is also the secret of their deep and abiding peace, the dynamic reality that is built on growth together rather than on a lifeless truce. If we look at lovers, or if we are fortunate enough to experience it in our own lives, we get some feeling for eternal life. Some people object to the notion of eternal life because it seems to project a numbing sameness of existence on the screen of the future. However, as we realize the true nature of love as a reciprocal activity in which each response deepens our sense of ourselves—making us more alive—we develop a sense not of the sameness but of the excitement of eternity. Love is the only thing that challenges what seems to be the final ending; it breaks and defeats death and turns its presumed victory into emptiness by the power of the resurrection. Love lets us know something of our abiding identity as God's children, whom he loved into life and by whose spirit we can see past all the temporary endings of our lives.

Going away for good

All the small separations and the need to be loving enough not to claw at life or at others as though we could make them our safe and unchanging possessions hint at and prepare us for a further mystery—that of death, all too often shunned, disguised, or otherwise looked away from for many generations. Death is a moment of significance to be weighed in the same scale with birth, an experience to complete our sense of meaning rather than to destroy it. Death must be seen in the context of all that we mean and share with each other. Far from being a door opening on nothing, death is filled with meaning, especially for those who have come to terms with the poignancy of going away.

In a recent interview psychiatrist Elisabeth Kübler-Ross suggested that the cultural taboos which keep children away from sickrooms and shielded from death also shield them from life. Children should instead be permitted, insofar as possible, to face and absorb the lessons that only the dying can teach us:

> For any child it is a blessing to be with a parent or grandparent in the process of dying. If you can, expose your children to old people who can be mean and grouchy and unbearably difficult, but also very beautiful, so that children know that beauty is not just nice makeup, but that an old wrinkled face can be just as beautiful. . . . Today we avoid exposing our children to dying patients like the plague. . . . How in the world can such children learn to accept death?

Dr. Kübler-Ross points to the fact that of all the opportunities we may have in life for riches and achievement, none exceeds those which ask us to penetrate the mysteries of our own humanity. Death has no hidden secrets from people who have come to terms with going away at earlier stages in life. Life terrifies those who have never been able to acknowledge and feel the simple mystery of separation. When we face into these squarely we come out of them as bigger, more alive, and more loving persons.

The great secret, of course, is that the multiple goings away of life never truly separate us or despoil us of what we have known and shared together. We can lose things—material treasures of all kinds—but the feeling for each other that we surrender—or offer as a sacrifice of love—when we must part adds to rather than takes away from our experience of life. We will never run out of separations from those we love, and the more we enter into them, the less power they, or death itself, will have over us. Death may not yet be a friend but it surely will not be a foe; it will be a place we have visited before, an experience we can pass through with a sense that we will not only survive but that we will do so in a richer and better fashion.

On failure

Success is big in America, but life is filled with failure. There is so much failure, in fact, that the Massachusetts Institute of Technology recently initiated a new course on failure as a "dominating theme in society." To fail is an experience we must all learn to understand and handle in order to lead any kind of human and Christian life.

Most of us do not need any reminders about the reality of large and small failures during the course of our lives. The faculty at MIT points out that not only do many institutions and services work poorly but that a fear of failure, whether it concerns school, business, marriage, or health, dominates the American imagination. It is small wonder that some persons, catching the tide right, have made a big success out of courses, books, and seminars which promise some immunity to failure in any or all of these endeavors. Helping people to master the mechanisms of success, whether in sexual relations or in avoiding arthritis, is a growth industry in the United States. There is something touching in the title of the huge bestseller, *I'm OK, You're OK*, a phrase that, in itself, builds our self-confidence by recognizing and absolving us of personal failure at one and the same time.

It is also striking that so many of society's institutions have been designed to deal with the pervasive reality of failure. Thus we have the courts, prisons, and legal escape hatch of bankruptcy, as well as welfare systems and insurance and multiplied medical plans. Failure seems a fundamental pattern of life, something through which we must live.

The academic doctors at MIT are divided on how to define failure. Some of the faculty members have suggested that a two-part definition be used. The first centers on "failure-bad," indicating those experiences that give rise to feelings of inadequacy and guilt in us; "failure-learn," on the other hand, describes the experience in which, through making a mistake, we enlarge ourselves by learning something.

These are familiar notions to anyone who has ever meditated on the meaning of success and failure in life. Some individuals, acclaimed as successes, suffer a special kind of failure during their lifetime—the failure to be appreciated. It is not so much that they fail in themselves or in their work; they find that they have been born "out of due time," and that the large masses of people around them are not yet ready to see life with the same vision they possess. This is often the fate of the poet or the artist, but it can happen to ordinary people as well. It is very difficult for people to keep trusting themselves when their visions and hopes go unrewarded.

What do you do?

Visionaries, even when they are just ordinary people with the sense of how things are changing around them, finally make some compromise between their ideal of success and their experience of failure. Those who insist on absolute success—such as some human potential movement advocates—sometimes demand an absolute freedom from any previous responsibilities or relationships in view of a new chance at self-fulfillment. In order to seek a new and better chance at success, people can give up not only their jobs but also the families they feel have trapped them into failure. These escapes destroy the context of life, that web of relationships and responsibilities that can never be successfully put aside in favor of making a judgment only in terms of our own needs. Life for everyone is finally a negotiated treaty that accepts failures and frustrations in order to make possible some reasonably important successes.

It is also important to keep a certain perspective on the things that are acclaimed as instant successes. Look back at the book and play reviews of only a year or so ago and ask yourself what has happened to many of these successes and those who designed them? Success is a dangerous experience, as many people have learned. To remember that Thursday's newspaper still wraps Friday's fish helps us all to keep things in perspective.

The stress of success

Making good is hard on many people. The very thing they seem to want, whether in business, the arts, or in some other public forum, brings with it a great burden, especially if such success is achieved early in life. It is rare, according to the people at MIT, to have a significant success without many previous failures. A long road leads to success for most people; it may be more of a process than a single event. If a person has an initial success, he or she is almost certain to fail because it is so difficult to follow up on a great triumph. Some people fumble success because their triumphs make them feel guilty. They feel uneasy about having made a lot of money or having achieved the acclaim that is denied to others. Success has the power to make them miserable.

Such seems to be the experience of the late novelist Malcolm Lowry, who wrote a poem about this experience after the success of his novel *Under the Volcano.* "Success," he wrote, "is like some horrible disaster, worse than your house burning, the sounds of ruination/as the roof tree falls following each other faster/while you stand, the helpless witness of your damnation.

. . ." It is a common experience that builds strange pressures into the lives of many persons who, as a solution, seek an unconscious path toward failure in order to lessen the weight of having succeeded. Some people, in other words, handle the stress of success by beginning an unconscious and finally successful courtship with failure.

Fear of failure

Fear of failure, along with cancer and heart attacks, should be listed as one of the great killers of human beings. It paralyzes persons on the cliff edge of life, causing them to hold back not only from success but even from experiencing some of life's ordinary sweetness. Psychological research, for example, shows that while some persons are motivated by the pleasure they take in success, others chart the course of their lives in order to avoid what they fear most, failure.

This research demonstrates that persons with a history of success tend to choose fairly realistic goals that they have a chance of reaching and enjoying; others who have a history of failure, however, characteristically set goals that are unrealistic. They choose objectives that are either too high or too low for them. What they eliminate by this maneuver is the risk of failure. When the goal is too low, they are sure of always succeeding but they never test themselves or their deeper possibilities. When the goal is too high, they are certain of failing. But nobody can blame them for it; they cannot be counted failures for having tried something that is so overwhelming in itself.

This effort to avoid the degradation of failure takes life away from persons, causing them to settle not for a sensible compromise about what can realistically be achieved, but for a mess of pottage that cannot nourish them but that will not make them sick, either.

The risk of loving, so often spoken about these days, is related to this kind of experience. If one fears failure and constructs a life-style to avoid it, he never even comes close to relationships that provide the reward of human intimacy. Intimacy is a bittersweet prize, however. It is the greatest experience we can have and yet one that knows failure and hurt. One cannot enter with his guard up; the self must be vulnerable in loving and being loved.

Death at LaGuardia Field . . .

Death visits the world savagely every day, as it once did most cruelly at LaGuardia Field. Death came for the travelers, in a dark wind of glass and steel cutting an instant forever out of time, burning it into our minds as it did into the shattered clocks of the airport. The images seem frozen in the second before death, and if we examine the scene we see some of the mystery of life that is always there, the liturgy of existence that is enacted in every homely moment, but that we, numb almost to wonder in simple things, do not usually sense.

For the treasures of life are never far from the surface wherever the mystery of travel is celebrated. It is harder to feel it in airports, whose hard angles and closed, stuffy spaces carry no hint of the sky they lay open for us. It is better felt in railroad stations, so much like old churches and with great distances and stained glass to provide a proper setting for the coming together and going apart that fill all our lives. It is not strange that old railroad stations were crowned with gods mistakenly identified as lords of commerce rather than of life; something soared in their aspiration, however, something profound struggled to emerge to mark the place where so much of what counts in life occurs.

We try to look away from the pain of separation, pretending that it never takes place or that it does not hurt so much when it does happen. But can we name a mystery more common than that of separation? And moments of travel, of hellos and goodbyes, stir it deep in the recesses of our unconscious. We are all touched by separation, and we do not know quite what to do about it. We cannot manage it out of our lives, and we do not like to keep it in focus. So we pull back from the LaGuardia explosion not only because of the tragedy there but because the blood of the travelers splatters on all of us. We are the travelers, the pilgrims whose lives are led in simple comings and goings, in separation and reunion, in ordinary passages in which we can look closely at ourselves and at the hinges of human relationship that bind our existence together.

For here were people beginning or ending Christmas visits as well as that secondary tier of travelers—those who drop off visitors or pick them up for another leg of their journey. Were they filled, as we so often are, with the feelings left over after a holiday, with the strange ambivalence that trails from anticipation and realization, from looking forward and looking back? What of the seventy-two-year-old woman waiting to meet a friend with whom she was to leave on a round-the-world trip? She had missed the first limousine to Connecticut and was waiting amid the drivers who would also die when the bomb went off. Or the eighteen-year-old Marine heading back to his base who missed his plane and lost his leg? And the mining engineer returning from a day's trip to the Midwest? There, too, stood a real estate agent, a design director, and a drugstore manager, some arriving and some waiting, all of them poised on one side or the other of the mystery of separation. Who can fail to wonder at the echoes in the newspaper description of another young man who was killed waiting for a limousine, "the only son of a widowed mother"; and who will raise him to life again?

It is a story we have all inhabited, of planes missed and buses delayed, and of finding ourselves waiting in unexpected places. But this cold clear night was different because all these persons had finished their journeys; their lives had a fullness we could see if we could look deeply into them. They had made a shape long ago of their existence against that windy darkness in which circuits were being aligned and passages were moving toward completion, where invisible lines were intersecting and events were drawing tight around this circle of people. For suddenly everything that had mattered had been said and done. They stood in that interlude of separation, on that fine edge, swaying like the bridge of San Luis Rey, where we make our own daily pilgrimages.

So the year ends

And what do we do about it? It gives us a chance to look more closely at the route we have come, to note the way stations of our pilgrimage, and to accept what has ended in our lives so that we can begin again in the new year. What has ended, especially in our human relationships, cannot just be shrugged off.

Sometimes, even if it is not death but only separation, we mourn it. I read recently of a college professor who suddenly recognized that when his daughter left for college something had ended that could never be taken up again in quite the same way. He noted that he had talked jokingly on the surface of not missing her but that inside himself something more profound had occurred. He had not lost her but the period of her child-hood—of her being a daughter in the house—was over. She was gone and, if the event were to have meaning for either, he had to let her go. And so he had to respect the meaning of that ending without denying its pain—and so make it possible for a new part of life to begin.

Not everything deserves mourning, of course, but the large events of being alive must be kept in clear perspective. To deny that certain periods of experiences of our lives are concluded is to blur our sense of what is going on. There is nothing more out of place, for example, than a middle-age man trying to dress and behave like his college-age son. There are few things more melancholy than the situation in which a dead person's room goes unchanged for years—everything as it was—as though he or she might return at any moment. These refusals to accept the many endings we must face and work through only compound our problems with living.

Otto Rank, the famous psychiatrist, wrote of the difference between "being separated" and "separating oneself." In the latter he saw evidence of the will to individuation. Our growth to our fullness depends on whether we can separate ourselves from the past or not. For, like it or not, we will be separated one way or another by circumstances anyway.

So it is with endings. We can actively separate ourselves from what is over and done with in our lives, or we can wait until providence does it, sometimes rudely, for us. Only if we can understand the mystery of ending and separation can we appreciate the fact that the last of December is a spiritual milestone for each of us. Only then can we glimpse some of the grandeur of the related mystery of beginning.

CHAPTER 4

A time to plant and a time to uproot the plant . . .

Giving up an adjustment

Well, a person says, I thought the whole idea in life was to achieve an adjustment. That is what the experts have been selling. That is what we are all working toward, a good adjustment.

Ah yes, but is a good adjustment all there is to life? Is it even the ideal? Or are we, curiously but persistently, always breaking out of adjustments, giving them up all the time in order to achieve better ones for ourselves? This is the law of the creative life, an existence that belongs to more than artists and poets.

We all create our lives, and nothing is more important in this than that moment in which we shake loose from the way we have always done things and take that leap toward a better and newer approach. This happens, for example, whenever an individual consciously changes jobs, especially later in life. There is a great deal of risk in giving up what is familiar, what can be counted upon, in order to pursue something that may prove only to be a dream. And yet it is the person willing to take that chance who usually makes more than a dream out of the new adjustment.

This is what happens when persons go into psychotherapy, ready to surrender a neurotic adjustment that, howsoever feebly, still manages to hold existence together for him or her, in order to find a new and better way of living. That is, indeed, what happens to artists shaking off past achievements in order to reach out toward a new vision of the truth. Poets speak of having to learn to throw themselves away if they are going to do anything but repeat themselves. They must allow their previous adjustment to die, in a very real sense, in order to reach the light.

When summer wanes, the earth shakes off an adjustment, a comfortable one of fruitfulness and fullness, one we are tempted to cling to and the passing of which we mourn as the days grow shorter. And yet it must be so if we are to reach the future. There is a season for everything, and the harvest cannot be attained without the surrender of the fullness of midsummer.

All of us make adjustments as we feel autumn approaching. We must get back to work, or on to a new project, or into a new school year, or any of a dozen other substantially new adventures. We have to give up something in order to make a sure journey into the future. We feel autumn's challenge like an ache in the bones. We must permit something we have grown comfortable with to die if we are going to reach the light.

Maybe we all need to inspect our present adjustment. Sometimes, even if we are not neurotic, we hold on to a psychological adjustment that works but doesn't get us very far. We are like people holding on to the railing against seasickness or a light pole against the wind. It's fine for holding on but it doesn't allow us to get anywhere.

Neurosis is an adjustment to the stresses of life and to our inner conflicts. It is ordinarily a bad, painful one, but it works. It is hard to give up an old adjustment and to enter into unfamiliar territory with our defenses down. That is the model we can all inspect as we feel the tug of the future inside us and know that the richness of our lives depends on whether we say yes to that future or try stubbornly to hold on to what so rapidly becomes our past.

Surrendering an old adjustment need not be as dramatic as working through a neurosis. It may just be giving up an old angle of vision, a fixated blind spot, a prejudice. These may just be other ways to describe what we mean by growth. We let go of something, unsure of how we will be as we reorganize ourselves around some new vision of our own possibilities. That's the kind of change to trust because it is built on something deep and true in ourselves. It is not the stuff of impulse, but the raw material for a richer life.

This is the kind of death to ourselves that is redemptive because it triumphs over fear and leads us into a genuine experience of resurrection. Where else do we taste resurrection except in a deepened and expanded sense of ourselves? How else do we communicate it to others except by a willingness to take the risk of expanding our relationships and giving up what we have grown comfortable with in order to find something richer and more human about each other. That's an autumn thought for a lifetime.

Letting go

It may be that the hardest thing to face about love is the fact that it never stops asking something from us. Love, in other words, does not repose like a trophy in the chambers of the heart; it is more like blood, nourishing us but demanding nourishment at the same time. Love gains strength from truths that don't seem to fit together at first glance. Item: People who long to possess each other must also learn to let each other go.

This takes a lot of love and it incorporates us powerfully into the living mysteries of incarnation, death, and resurrection. I am not sure that it ever gets any easier for people, even for those who understand it quite clearly. It may be the great, deep secret of lasting love, the very thing people are clamoring to discover, the kind of willingness to give up our claims on each other that makes us free and full as human persons. But some people don't find it because they are looking for something more complex and majestic.

Letting go is the opposite of another strategy that many persons use to protect their ravaged hearts—the noninvolvement syndrome by which friends stay clear enough of each other never to get snagged on each other's emotions. That works but it does not make love deeper; it only builds a higher wall around each one of us. Real lovers head right for each other's hearts, getting tangled in each other's feelings all along the way. This is why it is so difficult—so downright painful—to face the deaths of self that necessarily follow on coming alive to each other.

Love is seeded with this paradox all along its path; the more we want each other, the more we must be willing to respect each other's separateness. The more we would be sensitive to each other's needs, the more we must be willing to let each other go. Love means that we keep making room for the other to live in and that we surrender some of our space in order to do that. The biggest miracle of love is not that two persons dissolve into one but that, remaining distinct and contrasting as human beings, they can freely and gently share the treasures of their persons with each other.

We all like to think of things in the possessive case, but that attitude can destroy friendship and love more quickly than arguments about finances or in-laws. The person who honestly wants to love another does not sacrifice his or her natural liking or respect for the other. He must surrender something of a different order altogether, something whose roots go back down deep inside himself, his almost instinctive tendency to take and make others a part of himself. This only seems natural, you will undoubtedly say, something that is very much a part of ourselves, as much as wanting to stake a claim on one's own land or home.

That is why a genuine death to ourselves is involved in yielding up the things that make us want to close our hands possessively on persons around us. At a certain stage of love this is exactly what people want to do. They must, however, grow through this if they are to attain a deeper and more lasting kind of love. Ultimately, lovers free each other by acknowledging each other's individuality and giving each other the strength and the room to fulfill it.

We cannot free another person unless we are willing to cut through the chains by which we would make them fast to ourselves. Persons who love each other ride freely through life at each other's side; the public promises they make are not meant to shackle them together as much as to serve witness to the mystery of trusting freedom through which they remain alive to each other.

Letting go through putting to death our own urges to dominate the attention of another actually deepens the relationship instead of destroying it. When we can make a clean and unconditioned gift of life to each other we enter together into the mystery of resurrection, a realm we may only enter when our selfishness begins to die. Lovers empty themselves on each other's behalf, letting the other be separate and yet finding greater union within the other at the same time.

How does this work out in ordinary life? You do not need to look very far. Take the husband whose wife wants to return to school, for example, and all the small deaths he must be willing to accept in order to free her for this further opportunity. The deaths involved in letting another person go are not dramatic; they have as much to do with washing dishes and surrendering a comfortable routine as with anything else. Those freely accepted small deaths, however, enlarge life greatly.

A husband and wife must free each other—literally let each other go—when their work or other circumstances place them in contact with other men and women, the very situation in which jealousy can breathe withering dragon-fire all around. A measure of dying, in other words, goes into that special trusting through which man and woman share each other with the world around them, and those neighbors, friends, or associates who may need to draw on their strength for a while. This is the kind of expanded love that is not afraid of loving anything by giving itself away.

This latter kind of gift of man and woman to others begins at home, because exactly the same dynamic applies to the way love must enlarge itself to make room for children. When children are considered an intrusion on a married couple's relationship with each other, they will be treated that way. They can die of the emotional malnutrition caused by husbands and wives who have not learned to give each other away.

Letting another person go is the lesson that must be learned by a wide variety of loving persons: A teacher must die to his or her own self-interest, for example, in letting his or her pupils find their own way toward learning; a clergyman or a counselor must let his own wishes die in order to make sure that the freedom to move away on their own is available to those he helps.

Poverty of spirit comes down to this far more than it does to living in a hovel or giving away your shoes. Lady Poverty asks for hearts, for letting go of others not because we want to be detached (a fairly selfish motive) but because we need to be free. The wonderful part is that once we have learned to let go we discover that we can never again lose anything.

A meditation on Patty Hearst

It is the reverse fairy tale of the age, more flowering of evil in the California sunlight that fascinates everyone and gives a strange delight to the psychologically shrunken who curse their own deprivation and are nourished by the fall of the powerful and beautiful. And the princess had no knight to save her from her shame as she walked every day to her trial adorned with steel chains rather than gold bracelets. A long time will pass with the court adjourned and silent and the records sealed and stored away before we forget the images of the Hearsts during their nightmare years. And people will argue about the verdict and Steven Weed and the Hearsts themselves, past and present, without wondering how it all happened and whether any of the principals will ever be happy again.

During the time of the trial the *New York Times* described the deep changes that had taken place in Randolph and Catherine Hearst. "Acquaintances say they have been hurt by the events of the last two years as much, perhaps, as their twenty-two-year-old daughter. They sit in her courtroom every day now, sad and serious in their blacks and navy blues, two people who have retreated from the gay social life they once led, into recurring states of isolation and fear, even anger and bitterness."

Yes, one wonders, can anything ever be the same for them—

or between them—after the wrenching emotional forced march
of those many months? Where did it all begin and what business is it of ours, we ask, moving back from the tabloid head-
lines to the sad but compelling tale of estrangement across the
widening chasm of one short generation. How many Americans,
wanting to do the best thing, have found themselves gazing
across the same space, as puzzled as the Hearsts about how far
away everything familiar suddenly seems?

When did the scenario begin? For surely we watched only one
of the later acts. The pattern was set somewhere else, when
things were sunny and the differences didn't seem to matter or
were ignored. It was no accident that suddenly occurred, no
unpredictable fate that settled on the Hearsts like a cloud. No,
Patty got them into the courtroom, into the glare of the television lights, into the open for purposes no judge or jury will ever
quite be able to understand. Settling the case was one thing;
understanding the powerful family dynamics as acted out in
public is quite another.

We all make the shape of our lives quite early; we design our
destiny in and through the relationships of our lives. It comes
clear later, years later for most of us, but the big commitments,
the ones that determine so many of the later outcomes, these are
the ones we make at the very beginning of friendship and love.
We have the chance, over and over again, to change our direction with each other but we often fail to understand or we are
distracted or too self-absorbed. When we are blessed it is because we were generous and knowing—or others gave these
gifts of life to us—so that we have been able to travel on this
strength ever since. It is worth thinking about when we try to
understand ourselves and what we do to our own lives and to
the lives of those close to us.

It is never too late to learn, or to give more of ourselves, but
do we take the time or make the sacrifices? Or are we fated to
act out a story we wrote for ourselves long ago? Can we identify
with the questions raised by writer Elizabeth Cullinan in her
narrator who sees a sister of President Kennedy on a New York
street. "I got a sense, as I walked behind the couple, of how
events leave people stranded, how from a certain point in our

lives on—a different point for each life—we seem only to be
passing time. I thought of the Kennedys in Washington, the
Kennedys in London, the Kennedys in Boston and Hyannis
Port. Which were the important days? The days in the White
House? The days at the court of St. James's? Or had everything
that mattered taken place long before, on the beaches of Cape
Cod where we saw them sailing and swimming and playing
games with one another?" *(New Yorker,* Jan. 26, 1976, p. 34.)

Can you see spring come?

Some people say that you cannot see the seasons change, that it
all happens too slowly, and that we only feel the transformation
when it is completed. But such persons may be looking in the
wrong direction. Or even worse, they may not be looking at all.
The breaking up of winter ice makes me think about what we
see in the seasons and what we see in life itself. How sad it
would be if we could never see spring make its journey; it is
sadder still not to see the seasons of life in the people all around
us.

We live in a culture that has a preoccupation with surfaces,
with what we might term the sensuous aspect of things. The
lines of the surface are all-important, whether these are the bare
surfaces of human beings or the designs of our clothing and
cars. Some observers feel that such a fixation with surfaces is a
sign of narcissism, of a fundamentally undeveloped personality,
one that is caught up in its own coils and can never relate deeply
to anyone else.

Such a way of looking at things is, in the judgment of these
analysts, an immense block to being able to love or be loved.
That is why so many persons, despite their commitment to the
promises of a sensual age, come up empty and unhappy in the
long run. They think they have the right approach to life but,
somehow or other, it keeps coming unstuck, like a badly
wrapped gift.

There is no need to condemn or get mad at people who cannot
see outside themselves. Rather, one is moved by their isolation,
by that soul-biting aloneness that is far worse than loneliness.

At least when we are lonely it is because we are or were able to see someone else in his or her own identity and to respond to them for their own sake. Loneliness is what we feel when we can see outside ourselves; aloneness is what we suffer when we cannot.

This is why spring is a season for lovers; it is a time to see things clearly, to revel in their unique moments of progressive change and to sense hope in everything that is still rich and wonderful about the world and about other people. It is a season for believers who, breaking the spell of their own self-concern, can see deeply into life in all its forms. This is a time for shaking ourselves loose from the sleep that we may have allowed ourselves during a long winter. It is a time for seeing, a time for loving.

Van Gogh once wrote that despite everything else, "still a great deal of light falls on everything." The world, especially the world of other persons, reveals itself to us in that light all the time. Our problem may be that we have not looked, not even at the wondrous light, in a long time. We think we have seen everything so we travel on the crusted impressions of long-past seasons. We are bored with what is so familiar; we make our mark and pass on, cursing the sameness of our days.

But spring never comes the same way twice. And people are doubly filled with constant surprises. People, like spring itself, cry out all the time to be looked at freshly. Indeed, the basic meaning of the word "respect" is just that, the ability to look back at something, to view it again, to see it freshly. God knows we all need spring, not just for its final warmth and flowers, but for its epic lesson in appreciating the long small miracle of steady growth in which we are all implicated. The simple condition for seeing spring and life itself is that we look up from our own concerns for a while. When we discover this, a great deal of light still falls on everything.

Do I make any difference?

This is a big and extremely difficult question for many people at the present time. Does my life have any significance? Or is it just part of a vast tumbling array that has less shape than historians would have us believe. Terrible questions, these, and yet they are asked often in the midst of what Matthew Arnold described a century ago as "this strange disease of modern life."

Nobody needs to be instructed about the events and experiences that force these questions on people; all I dread, a contemporary Will Rogers might say, is what I read in the papers. And numerous prophets are telling us that the worst is yet to come. It is bad enough that we encounter uncertainty in the very institutions—church, state, and education—that are supposed to reflect and uphold our values; but it is worse when these traditional values are doubted and mocked all around us. Can people really love each other? Can it ever last a lifetime? And what is the sense of being truthful when nothing seems to operate in a truthful manner? People wonder about trust and honor and whether anybody believes in fidelity anymore.

Beyond this, however, there are the mounting crises of famine and poverty and the wars and rumors of wars yet unreported from a world that the average person does not seem able to touch or to change effectively in any way. These great and tragic events seem to be locked away even from those who care and want to do something about the world and its problems. But how do you do it as the news of disaster upon disaster piles up and we become more discouraged about our capacity to affect the course either of the world or of our own lives.

It is a desolation for the spirit to live in the midst of so much need and to feel operationally powerless to make much difference. It is not that people don't want to make a difference; it's just that they are not sure that they can anymore.

Contemporary frustrations

People experience frustration on many levels. They seem to have more longing than realization of their hopes, more plans than achievements. There is a special frustration, for example, connected with wondering whether human beings ever do truly reach each other. Do people meet or are they doomed always to be strangers to each other? You don't have to be young to ask this question, which can stalk the dreams of couples long married. It is not one they are likely to speak out loud readily. How threatening to pose a question that raises the possibility that they never have reached each other, that they have only been in touch with outward impressions that have long since been transformed or disappeared altogether. This question is built on the worst of potential frustrations. We wonder if anybody else knows or cares about what we are really like. We know, for example, that there are things we have never shared with anybody; have we ever really gotten inside people we think closest to us? Or are we left to be lonely bearers of frustration the way some bear typhoid, to remain unconsoled in a world where things happen to us and where the control of our destinies, large and small, seems constantly to escape us.

One of the many consequences of frustration is apathy. Sometimes frustrated people get angry and smash things, but it is also possible for them to pull back into a hazy world of their own, to withdraw from human activity, to give up and let the imperfect world roll on without their participation. One is reminded of the cartoon character who said, "I don't know what apathetic means and I couldn't care less." Apathy becomes a defense against the complex and cruel challenges of contemporary life. This happens not only in regard to historic issues but, sadly enough, it is the kind of adjustment that many people make in their ordinary lives. They seem inwardly defeated and unable to respond with any freshness in life. Such persons feel they no longer make a difference in the relationships that, in fact, do make all the difference in their existence. Apathy is not a way out of the problem; it is just a poor adjustment to the hardest question we know.

Continuing truths

People can be helped to face and work through the frustrations of the age—to do more than stand there and let life happen to them—especially if they remember some of the following truths:

Heightened moments in life are very few. The moments in which we feel fully in tune and inspired occur rarely for most people. When they do happen, of course, they are extremely supportive because they justify the efforts we put into everyday life. Such experiences underscore and allow us to celebrate the rightness of our commitment as well as the soundness of the direction in which we are moving. But they are like the experience mountain climbers sometimes have after a long and arduous ascent. The sweet moment of triumph is fleeting. There is no place to go, literally, but down, back to the valley and to the struggles that are far more common than the moments of triumph. We will seldom, for example, have the feeling that we can directly affect some huge problem. That should not, however, diminish our willingness to work in small and persistent ways at trying to contribute to their solution. There may even be few heightened moments in friendship and love. For the most part there is the long steady climb, the heart of which is the effort that cannot be separated from the quiet joy of moving through life closely with another person. It is being with somebody through the climb that counts.

Direct participation in large and exciting events is denied to most people. Even jet-setters, beautiful people, and other assorted celebrities are hardly ever close to genuinely important happenings. Their lives look interesting from a distance but, close up, jet-setters frequently lack even the basic satisfactions that come to more ordinary people; they are too busy trying to be important to understand the peace that comes with being ordinary, and that is why their lives are more search than discovery.

Most of us can do more than we think we can. Frustration, to some extent, is a function of our failure to realize how much extra energy and time we have at our disposal. Most married people, for example, could involve themselves in a worthwhile civic project even though they protest that they do not have any time for it. More significant, even, is the fact that they could actually have more time for each other if they only looked around and discovered it. Time for good things does not have to be bought; it only has to be discovered because it is always there.

Do what you can do, an old adage says, *instead of dreaming about what you cannot do.* This works in human relationships as well as in regard to civic, religious, or other concerns. Anytime we find ourselves musing, "Wouldn't it be nice if . . ." This is firsthand evidence that we are building a defense against action. There is usually something constructive that we can do and it usually concerns ourselves. As Dr. William Glasser, author of *Reality Therapy,* notes, "While we're waiting around for other people to change around us, our soundest course of action is to change something about ourselves." This is something we can always do and it beats waiting for better luck, for the intervention of angels, or for other people to transform themselves. When we change ourselves in relationship to others this makes a difference—others then respond differently to us because we have restructured the relationship. This is a key to overcoming the frustration that we too often think we are powerless to overcome.

Nothing doesn't count

To those who understand human relationships there is really no moment and no event that can be described as merely casual, insignificant, or even neutral as far as all other relationships go. The stuff of human relationships is largely invisible. The dimensions of friendship and love cannot be seen, much less measured. The space between people is a sacred territory, however, and any movement within it, howsoever slight, does make a difference. We always have an effect on each other, even at the moments in which we wish that we did not.

That is what is at the heart of fidelity, for example, a virtue that sounds oddly old-fashioned in a contemporary world where being unfaithful, we are constantly told, doesn't seem to make any difference at all. Ah, but it does! Things can never be the same—people only like to think that they are—when persons have not been truthful about their lives with each other. Whether we are true to ourselves and to those we love makes the biggest difference of all. It changes the energy balance of the universe and, in the long run, may contribute one way or another to the larger problems of the world to a far greater extent than we would like to acknowledge. What we are like, who we are as husbands, wives, teachers, or friends—all that together works toward making the world better or worse. We do touch larger affairs when we live with integrity in all the small experiences of our own lives. Otherwise the universe is a broken clock and we are not connected at all. Our experience tells us that we are always connected.

In the long run, we live in the midst of things we cannot see all the time, of effects we cannot measure and of commitments to outcomes that we may never be able fully to enjoy. Such notions are not only relevant to fidelity; they constitute a large part of the meaning of faith itself. To live as believers introduces hope into human affairs again. It rejects cynicism and all the unsatisfying substitutes to which people turn when they give up in the face of frustration. We do make a difference every time we commit ourselves in faith to each other, to our children, or to anyone who needs the investment of our belief in them. The world changes not when we dream about it but when we believe in it and make that clear in the everyday experiences of our lives.

There is something we can do, then, in our own way and in accord with our own gifts and possibilities. Call it being true to ourselves or being brave, or still believing when everything seems in doubt. We challenge the people who question love, for example, not by trying to sidestep the commitments of friendship and love but by taking them on. It is only an illusion to think that we can save ourselves from hurt or stress by not making any promises to each other. It is a tragic misreading of life to stay at the edges of love because we feel that it is a circle of danger in which we might be lost.

We make a difference, finally, by not being afraid to make a difference to someone else. Usually we hold back from this not because it is impossible—but because it is possible and we know it. We also know the cost of affirming life through love and real friendships, and that is the price we haggle over or try to avoid paying altogether. Whether we make a difference lies not in the secret fates but in our own hands.

The saddest words

Arrogance has been designated the sin of the age; you hardly count as a sinner these days unless you indulge in some arrogance. The more sophisticated speak of it as *hubris* but they still mean a wrongheaded, self-centered, and insensitive way of conducting one's life. Hubris is discussed as a species of pride, a famous old vice that, after several slow seasons, is coming back into our consciousness again. You can prepare yourselves now: Preachers, writers, and scores of repentant politicians will alternatively confess to and condemn arrogance over the next several months. That's the genius of arrogance; it is a marvelous-sounding sin and something worth being sorry about.

The only problem is that most people are not arrogant. They are, in fact, just the opposite, and this causes them intense pain. People are far more timid than they are arrogant and far more uncomfortable with themselves than they are overbearing with others. Rather than wanting to dominate the stage of attention, they draw back, fearing that there may not even be room for them in the wings. Many people, clutching their souls like dangerously billowing nightgowns, are afraid that others are going to see them for what they are in their own eyes. They say, in effect, "If you really knew me, you wouldn't like me."

These, I submit, are the saddest words of tongue or pen, far sadder than "it might have been." The sadness is more intense because these persons should have something more than regrets about life's mischances. They are, in many ways, people who are yet to be, people who have still not tasted much of the sweetness of life or love. Such persons are filled with a mixture of longing for something more than guilt at being so much less than they wish. The problems connected with self-esteem are enormous for a great many people, and their difficulties are only compounded when we make arrogance the sin of the month.

They are, unfortunately, ready to convict themselves of almost anything we can indict them with. Their souls are like litmus paper that reacts to undifferentiated guilt; they live like people ready to confess to whatever they are accused of.

Why do they feel this way?

People with low self-esteem try to look away from themselves, but they find that this is almost impossible. Uneasiness rides with them all the time, souring moments that they should enjoy and making them hold back from experiences they should enter. One is reminded of the wife of a British novelist who may have spoken for many of the people who lack confidence in themselves when she said, "For me heaven is a place where I won't have to be shy anymore."

A lack of healthy self-confidence is frequently a function of the way other people have treated these persons during their lifetime. We know that parents, for example, can have powerfully formative effects on their children's self-confidence through the attitudes they communicate toward them even very early in life. Children who do not feel good about themselves often have parents who do not feel good about them either. When, for example, adults make impossible expectations on the behavior of their children, they sentence them to a lifetime of low self-esteem. Whatever feelings we have about ourselves originate in the feelings others have toward us.

Learning plays a big role in assembling our personal psychological picture of ourselves. Self-confidence is not broken in one learning experience; it is gradually destroyed through a multitude of frustrated efforts to please people who simply cannot be pleased no matter how great our effort. It is important to understand the role of learning in this process, not only to explain how we acquire negative attitudes toward ourselves but also because whatever has been learned can also be unlearned. This is a source of hope for people who do not like themselves and feel that as a result, no one else can like them either.

Some people who are uncomfortable about themselves feel that way because they think they are the worst persons who have ever come along. There hasn't been any contest in this regard; in fact, all the entries have not come in and there would probably be a lot of ties for first place anyway. The persons of lowered self-confidence are not, as a matter of fact, terrible individuals at all. They are usually frightened by things that are fairly normal and acceptable, the kinds of things that other persons have been able to learn to live with. Sometimes the images that come to these people in their fantasies or the impulses that come to them in their feelings seem very terrible indeed. All people are capable of experiencing strange messages inside themselves; it is a characteristic of the human situation. Hardly evidence of depravity, this is more a signal of humanity. Nonetheless people who do not like themselves use this as firsthand evidence of their badness.

People of low self-esteem, despite abundant proof sometimes to the contrary, do not think that they are attractive, intelligent, or capable of achieving very much on their own. If they do something good or get some praise, they write it off as merely luck or an accident. It could never be something that they deserve for themselves.

This brings us to the chief feeling that these individuals experience about their own persons. They simply do not believe that they could be liked by other people just for themselves. They do not expect good treatment from others because it is so difficult for them to imagine that there is anything that others could find worthwhile in them. This makes relationships with others a difficult kind of thing. They mistrust other people because they feel that anybody who does like them must have some outside reason for doing this. These others must want something out of them because they could never be responding just to them. Those low in self-esteem frequently pull back from others or so stylize their relationships that they have little depth; they won't let those who like them get a close look at them for fear they will change their minds.

Bad advice

You have all heard others trying to cajole some person out of the
way he or she feels. "Come now, you don't really feel that
way," they will say, whether the person is grieving, irritated, or
frightened at taking an exam. The fact is, however, that people
really do feel the way they tell us they do, and no amount of
persuasion can argue against the facts of the matter. That is one
of the fatal dangers of trying to talk people out of their problems. Such an approach is built on denying that they have the
kind of problem they are actually describing for us. So it is with
people who lack self-confidence. Sometimes friends do attempt
to talk them out of this low view of themselves by pointing to
their accomplishments or telling them that other people really
do like them and that they cannot possibly feel the way they do
about themselves. This may make things worse instead of better, because these people are indeed emotionally convinced that
their feelings about themselves are justified. Reasoning with
them simply rubs salt in their wounds.

Perhaps more cruelly than anything else, modern advertising
plays on the uncertainties and self-distrust of persons by prom-
ising them social and business success if they use a certain
toothpaste, drive a certain car, or smoke those funny little
brown cigars. These are manipulations of people, ways of prey-
ing on their weaknesses for commercial gain. Someday we will
be wise enough to understand that it is sacrilegious to mistreat
people in this way. No product creates self-confidence, no answer from the *"Playboy* Advisor" makes for social success; nothing but coming to terms more deeply with oneself can redeem
persons from this deep lack of self-confidence.

What can we do?

Besides avoiding the kinds of mistakes which are based on ap-
proaches that do not take these people or their problems seriously, we must be prepared to be patient and accepting with
them. We usually want to push them from the outside and try

to buck them up by slapping them on the back and urging them forward into behaviors that make them very uncomfortable. If, however, we are ready not to do the wrong things in relationship to people who lack self-confidence, we may be able to do some of the right things, like letting them talk in their own words and at their own pace about their feelings toward themselves. We may not be able to talk them into feeling better about their own personalities, but as we listen and they talk, they may discover truths they could never come upon except in an unhurried and understanding atmosphere.

We can always give the gift of time. The unspoken message that goes with this gift is that they are worth it and that we are not counting the minutes or punching some time clock. They learn something when others have time for them and do not pressure them to prove themselves within certain time or space limitations.

We can love these people. It is well known that there are certain qualities that have to be loved out of us. There is just no other way they ever come into being. We can't talk people into feeling better about themselves but, with the kind of respect and concern that go with real love, they may feel that they are loved deeply and for themselves for the first time in their lives. Something comes to life in people when this experience occurs, something rich and profound that allows them to look at themselves in a new way because they suddenly feel that they are truly lovable. There is no way to design this, program it, or convince people of it. It is a wondrous experience that takes place unfailingly when one person reaches out in loving concern and commitment to another.

We can help these people by believing in them. An act of belief is always directed toward the future. It is not aimed at regrets about what might have been because faith's whole meaning is directed toward what can yet be, toward what persons can become in the future. A genuine commitment in faith returns the possibility of life to persons who need it very much.

That is why faith is not some dead insistence on something said or promised long ago. It is far livelier and it is only communicated by human beings, by real believers.

As we believe in and love others, they are gradually freed from the fears and uncertainties they have had about themselves because they no longer need to experience them. They no longer need to prove that they are worth the attention of others because they have suddenly won it without trying. Their defenses—their need to be busy, for example—drop away and they stand at last as they truly are with greater ease and freedom. It is a rebirth and a wonderful thing to see. It is even better to remember that we can participate in giving people back their lives all the time. There are people all around us just waiting for someone to respond to them now and to love out of them the true self that has been waiting timidly for years to be born.

Loose ends

Sometimes life seems to have more loose ends than anything else. There is, of course, something annoying about a loose end, whether it is on a sweater, a skirt, or the human spirit. We like wholeness and a sense of completion; loose ends depress us and make us uneasy. There is, in fact, an observable tension—more obvious in achievers than in nonachievers—to return to and to finish incomplete tasks. Psychology calls this the *Zeigarnik effect*, the urge able people feel not to leave things hanging. Most people who read this will identify in a glow of self-satisfaction with the achiever who gets things finished. But not everybody is like this. There are those we can call . . .

Loose enders

Some people settle, as students in college sometimes will, for an Incomplete in life. These include *the great beginners*, who flush quickly with a variety of enthusiasms but who do not follow through on many projects and end up with a collection of half-completed endeavors. They have open hobby kits gathering dust in the cellar, notes for an unfinished article or a book somewhere on the top of their cluttered desks, barely used skis in the closet, and a bookmark in chapter three of *War and Peace* still glaring at them from the bookshelf. Such lives are filled with beginnings, almost-events, not-quite accomplishments, and things that might have been.

These are signs to read carefully, if we discover them in our lives, before we end up on the margin of life in semipermanent mourning for the things we never did get around to doing, the chances we decided not to take, and the sense of satisfaction we never quite experienced. Such difficulties may be related to a basic problem of personal identity that cannot be overcome by willpower or even by prayer and fasting. It takes steady insight into one's personality to realistically label one's own talents and possibilities. Some people never finish anything because, right from the start, they overestimate themselves and what they can accomplish. It is almost as common for people to underestimate themselves and to hold back from the kinds of risks that are as necessary as breath and heartbeat for a true sense of life.

There are loose ends connected with *things we do not get said* before our relationships end; people leave us, and the situation becomes irretrievable. There are things we do not get written in our letter or inscribed on our cards, a fullness of our hearts that we know we have never put quite the right way to the person deserving this message about our affection. Our life is full of saying things like, "I always wanted to tell him how much I admired him . . ." or "I always wanted her to know how much she has helped me in my life. . . ." Maybe these loose ends are why the greeting card business thrives, why we have testimonial dinners, and why sometimes it is a good idea to send a gift even when it is not somebody's birthday. These express the kinds of things we have not said well enough about the richest and best loves of our lives.

A loose-ended list

There is, in fact, a long list about the loose ends of our existence. If we cannot banish them, we can learn to read their messages and to live more comfortably with them. Living with loose ends may be as good a way of defining life as we presently have. We should not be surprised to find them in ourselves or in others. We do well, in fact, to leave room for them. If loose ends demand patience, they also demand that we have a sense of timing about the right moment to handle them for ourselves or for those close to us. They cannot be abruptly sheared off or tucked in so that they make a good appearance even though they are still tangled up. They need care, the kind of human response that is at once powerful and understanding.

Life's loose ends are informative. They teach us about ourselves if we but inspect them carefully. They tell us, after all, something about what we consider important. They reflect in miniature our scale of values and, as we try to trace them down, we get closer in touch with our own basic personalities. The loose ends lead back to ourselves; there should be no great fear attached to looking closely at them.

Loose ends give us potent clues about our basic incompleteness as human beings, about our need for each other, and about a fulfillment that lies finally beyond all the loose ends of our existence. Loose ends are not live wires waiting to electrocute us. They are signals that enable us to understand our own journey and the powerful longing for a deeper sharing with each other that we will only experience in the full life waiting for us beyond what seems to be the last loose end of our existence.

CHAPTER 5

---

*A time to kill and a time to heal
A time to tear down and a time to
build up . . .*

Many ways to murder

Someday we will be wise enough to understand that there are many ways in which we can destroy a human being. We do not have to take away life with a bullet or a knife or a bomb. There are subtle ways, for which no one will even be tried in a court but which, nonetheless, take the breath and life out of a person as surely as any lethal instrument. We can kill people by denying them hope, by refusing to believe in them or by actively removing the possibilities for their future. There are many ways to do this:

Do not use a person correctly; fail to recognize his or her talents. Or be so jealous of someone you are afraid to let that person use his or her talents as fully as God intended.

Be insensitive to other persons, shielding yourself and your heart so completely that there is never any room for others. Be self-absorbed, in other words, and you will put lots of people to death, especially those closest to you. Worse still, you will never understand what has happened to you, or what you have done.

Starve a person, not physically but by denying him or her the truth that is necessary for understanding and finding the future.

Overprotect persons, shielding them against the dangers of life, and you will almost surely sentence them to psychological death.

Confuse someone about love, spouting cheap rhetoric that is easy to speak but impossible to take back. Confuse a person when he or she is young so that it is hard for that person to get it straight later on in life. Do this and you have scattered the fire that lights and warms life.

Get a person things and amusements; keep someone in the shallows so that he or she can never get near the hope that is only found out in the deeper water. This person will never know what life is at all; people treated this way will have been put to death before they have understood the meaning of being alive.

Violence comes when we have no words

We all remember the story of Billy Budd, the innocent seaman in Herman Melville's novel. Psychologist Rollo May has pointed out the profound significance of Billy's reaction when the ship's master, Claggart, brings charges against him; Billy is so stunned that he can only stammer. He strikes out and kills the man who would corrupt him and so he must hang for his deed. In his defense, however, he says: "I did not mean to kill him. If I could have found my tongue I would not have struck the blow." Here, indeed, we are helped to understand the final failure of those who do not understand the importance of the right words for our experience. When we cannot speak of our feelings we are possessed by their fury.

Persons who abandon the effort to communicate in words step backward to draw on the primal forces that surge up from the irrational. Many blows are struck in this way; violence seems to have its way with those who cannot or will not find their tongues. Small wonder that some have speculated on whether the world will end in fire or ice; there is a pull in the irrational but it draws us toward that violent fate in whose shadow we are persons no more.

Standoff

Life is filled with standoffs—those situations that are not quite defeats but that are by no means victories. Standoffs are like chemical compounds that have not quite jelled; they are made up of hope that is still held on to and of resignation that is not quite accepted, of the ideal and the real actively resisting any effort to blend them. Standoffs are a species of frustration, and they sound in our lives as regularly as churchbells. F. Scott Fitzgerald, the famous novelist, quoted an Egyptian proverb in one of his notebooks which catches some of the feeling of life's standoffs: "The worst things:/To be in bed and sleep not,/To want for one who comes not,/To try to please and please not."

Standoffs are like the ache in arthritic bones; their very nature makes them hard to get at or to do anything about except try to live with them. Creation's storehouse is well stocked with situations that cannot be resolved, mysteries that fight being cleared up, as well as the tiny bones of experience as surprising and numerous and almost as invisible as those that hide in a fish dinner. And they stick in one's throat the same way. All these are aspects of what the poet Robert Frost once called our "lover's quarrel with life." We can inspect them under these headings:

Problems with ourselves.   Most of these concern our plans or hopes about the things we want to achieve in life. The standoffs come when we run up against our limitations and our youthful dreams become slightly mottled and need to be revised.

We face standoffs with ourselves when the very thing we had hoped for so earnestly remains beyond our open grasp. Or when illness, bad luck, or a transfer of jobs suddenly sends our dreams skittering away from us like a beachball on the windswept sea. There comes a point when we can seem to go no further, no matter how sincere our efforts or how worthy our vision of accomplishment.

This can also happen when we seem to run out of give, when fatigue or routine robs us of our capacity to keep going either at home or at work. As a result, we pull back from the activities of life for a while in order to recoup our strength. A standoff always causes us to pause because there is nowhere else to go; we have come too far to turn back; however, for the moment at least, progress is also blocked.

Problems with others.   This is our richest source of standoffs, of course, and it is also the area of our lives in which we feel the pressure of standoffs most keenly. Standoffs with other people hurt as much as anything we know. They occur in many different situations and they include the following:

A classic standoff occurs when people do what we don't want them to do—and sometimes this is even what they don't want to do themselves. The motives for these actions can be quite tangled, but the clash of wills, whether across the coffee table or across the generations, often precipitates an outcome that we simply cannot control or do anything about. We have to let go of it for a while because no matter how sure we are of our position, we simply cannot bring it into reality.

There are standoffs aplenty for young lovers as they try to make their way toward a relationship of mutual understanding and affection. There are many difficult passes to cross in this growth together, and the standoffs—some of them defensive and some of them sensible—are the chief reason that the course of true love does not run smoothly. They add something, however, to our experience of growth with each other, a lesson in patience and mutual appreciation that cannot otherwise be learned. Standoffs also give people time to see whether they are really ready for marriage or to see whether their friendship can stand various tests, like that of separation.

There are other standoffs between long-time friends and lovers as well. They are a mix of disagreements, misunderstandings, and even reasonably and unreasonably hurt feelings. They cause an impasse in relationship, however, across which neither party can travel for a while. Things simply get too hot to touch or too tender to probe, and the individuals involved can do nothing but back away and regard each other from a distance. This is not exactly the same as a retreat, but it is frustrating when, with the persons with whom we feel we should be most completely ourselves, we feel that communication has been interrupted.

Problems with things or other vague aggregates. These standoffs are increasingly part of our everyday life. Sometimes we can smile about these things, but it is very difficult to do so when we are in the midst of some frustrating situation with a machine that will not work no matter how much we tinker with it, a postal service that seems to hide the mail that we are looking for most, or a computer-hearted business that remorselessly sends us bills that we have already paid.

Houses or apartments can generate a standoff as well. They seem almost like living things in the way that they can time their successive breakdowns, spreading them out over the years so that although the repairs need not all be made at once, no breathing time is allowed between any of them. If you have ever heard anybody say, "Keeping this house up has taken the best out of me," you know the awesome power of things to throw us into the standoff position.

The lessons of standoff

As indicated in some of the points just mentioned, standoffs are not the worst things that can come along in life. If anything, they are tests of our capacity to believe and hope and carry on, or to come realistically to terms with life and ourselves. A standoff, after all, buys us time, the very thing that we need in certain situations. Take the difficulties we can have with those who are closest to us—our friends and loved ones. Family life is filled with standoffs; there may, in fact, be nothing more common. Show me a household in which everybody is speaking sweetly and reasonably to everybody else for more than twenty-four hours in succession, and I will yield the point. It is not surprising to find these situations, especially between people who live in the intimate range with each other. They know each other's faults and virtues, and the standoff may be a necessary psychological device to prevent more murders than already occur.

The interlude of the standoff enables things to cool down, much in the way they are supposed to do when impasses are reached in labor and other negotiations. This newfound time has many advantages because it keeps us from making things worse by pushing ahead with our viewpoint or argument at a time when its chances of being heard are minimal. It keeps us, in other words, from making things that are bad turn even worse.

The standoff also permits us to see ourselves and the person with whom we are experiencing some difficulty in much better perspective. When we have to move back from each other for a little while, we almost always improve our view. Standoffs give us the chance to do that, and unless we clamp our eyes shut tight in defiance, the better picture we see of each other is bound to help us reach each other again more lovingly when communication is renewed.

It is probably not bad to ask ourselves, in the space in which we wait during a standoff, what we are really trying to achieve anyway. When we cannot get what we want, we have an opportunity to reassess both our goals and our capacity to attain them. This may lead to a revised decision that, in the long run, will lead us to a happier and better life. The young man, for example, who cannot get the courses he had planned on or who is turned down by the graduate school he had hoped to attend may take another look at his plans to see whether they were not somewhat idealistic in the first place. The standoff can lead to a redesign of his plan in life much more in accord with what he can successfully and happily achieve.

Is it so bad if nobody wins once in a while? That is the natural outcome for a time of standoff. Everything is held in place for a while, and the struggle, no matter how much energy went into it, goes unresolved. This is the classic standoff, the kind that the United States found in Southeast Asia. Because of it, we have had long and deep thoughts about ourselves, our institutions, and our notions of what we can reasonably expect to achieve for the rest of the world. That it has been sobering and maturing for us as a people does not redeem the loss of so many young men, but it has added to our realism about our power and its possibilities.

The same kind of thing happens to each one of us, especially if winning becomes all-important in our lives. Despite the ridiculous exultation of it, winning is not everything and sometimes it is nothing at all. It adds up to zero when we win unfairly or without consideration for the rights and feelings of others or when we use power that has been severed from principle. A tied game does not settle anything even though it is entered into the record book. These situations are worth studying, because we learn a great deal when we can face the fact that there are situations in which we cannot win decisive victories over other people, in which we do not always have to demonstrate that we are right, and in which we do not have to prove over and over again how strong or smart we are.

A good standoff lets us see something of the illusion that is part of many of our victories. It can also lead us to a realization of how much we can lose of ourselves and of our integrity when we desperately have to win. There is food for meditation in any standoff; each one helps us see how human we are and how much we need each other and how few are the total victories in any form of life.

A sense of realism

Standoffs are worthwhile if we come out of them wiser; if we can fashion a better definition of ourselves, one that is closer to reality, one that puts us in better touch with ourselves and, therefore, in much better touch with everyone around us.

Standoffs allow us to love ourselves a little better and, therefore, make it easier for others to love us as well. Standoffs help us surrender arrogance and the destructive kind of pride through which we fill the sky with our own image and make very little room for other people. There is hard learning connected with standoffs and the frustrations they generate, but we never really lose anything when we give up what was false and selfish about us in the first place.

Humility is a virtue that is not spoken of very much anymore. After all, ours is a century of self-assertion, a time to rediscover and insist upon our rights and our own individuality. All this is well and good, but it is only beneficial if it is tempered with the kind of humility that is built on a realistic vision of ourselves. That is all that humility asks of us anyway: that we live in accord with the truth about ourselves and that we try to pursue, as Thomas Aquinas reminds us, our own excellence in a reasonable way. Life is studded with the standoffs that help us develop that humility or regain it if we have cast it aside. Standoffs are worthy of a prayer of thanksgiving because, although they are reminders of our weakness, they also point to our real strength. God doesn't ask much more from us than that we try to live with our own truth and our own talents. Maybe that is why the meek end up inheriting the earth.

The department of defenses

It has been very fashionable over the last several years to challenge people about their defenses. Getting at the truth, or what people take for the truth, has become the prize in reporting, in some species of community building, and in the first-person public confession. But everything that is brutal or scandalous is not necessarily the truth, and not every defense mechanism is bad for us. The soul can be demolished by the unwise and untimely shedding of all defenses, especially on the oversimplified grounds that they are defenses and so must be yielded up in the interest of the New Truth. But is the real truth about us found when we have given up adjustive mechanisms that may be indispensable to our best functioning and that are well integrated into our personalities?

There are, in short, mature defenses that are recognized as such by psychology which we should be able to openly acknowledge and not feel ashamed if, in fact, we employ them ourselves. One of the things that many pseudopsychologists do not seem to understand is the very real need for defenses in healthy persons. The defensive pattern tells quite accurately whether we are narcissistic, immature, or neurotic; it also informs us about our maturity.

Immature defenses

We may recognize healthier defenses if we first have some familiarity with those that are immature. These include the following patterns:

Acting out. This is well described by its name, for it refers to overt behavior that directly expresses unconscious wishes or impulses. Classically it is observed in persons who have not learned how to postpone gratification. They give in to their impulses, literally acting them out, because they cannot bear the tension that accompanies postponing their expression. Making a scene, having a fight—these are examples of acting out.

Hypochondriasis. And, as they say, there is a lot of this going around. Most people do not know about the psychoanalytic interpretation of their perceived aches and pains. In fact, most people think that hypochondriacs are phonies of a sort. Actually, hypochondriacs are translators who take some inner conflict and express it in a disguised form. It may be the "transformation of reproach toward others—arising from bereavement, loneliness, or unacceptable aggressive impulses—into self-reproach and complaints of pain, somatic illness, and neurasthenia" (*Comprehensive Textbook of Psychiatry*, 2nd Edition. Baltimore: Williams & Wilkins Co., 1975, Vol. 1, p. 535).

And what, you ask, do people get out of this? They may be able to avoid responsibility and guilt, among other things. The defense allows for regressive behaviors—for being cared for like a child—and, while it works, it is clearly immature.

Passive-aggressive behavior. If you have ever wondered why the car ahead of you on a two-lane road manages to move so slowly and piles up a long line of traffic behind it, you have probably been in at least remote contact with somebody's passive-aggressive defenses. In essence, these consist in expressing aggression indirectly toward others not by doing something but by failing to do something. The individual who does not show up for the meeting, the clerk who makes change very slowly despite the long line—these are examples of the immature defense of passive aggression. And there is a lot of this going around, too.

Projection. A handy if immature mechanism because through its use we are able to handle the feelings within ourselves that we cannot admit to or deal with directly. We attribute them to others—project them as we would a slide of our flawed psyche on a screen. Then it is permissible for us to be irritated by the quality that is no longer our own but somebody else's. This plays a big part in prejudice of all kinds. It also permits people to avoid closeness through excessive suspiciousness, blowing up minor problems into major ones, and other similar maneuvers. People who use projection frequently seem to be those looking for an argument. When you sense this as a pattern of relationship, you develop a feel for the immature nature of the defensive system, and you also understand why being sweet and reasonable to some people never works.

Regression. Frankly regressive behavior is the immature defense through which persons can avoid the conflicts or anxieties of the present by moving back to a style of behaving that fits a previous period in life. It is a literal journey backward to a technique of relationship that had been given up but is now reemployed. Thus, the grown-up who suddenly reverts to an immature solution for present worries offers us an example of regression. Using pouting, for instance, or some equivalent of taking the bat and ball and going home are examples of this defense in action. Almost anything that prompts the reaction "Stop being childish!" also fits.

Schizoid fantasy. This is the use of fantasy to deal with present conflicts or difficulties. It offers dreamy gratification through psychologically stealing away to a world in which the individual can write and direct the screenplay of his or her own life. Obviously such a retreat leaves problems unchanged in the real world.

So what?

What are we to make of something we have always known—that people can be immature; that even we, believe it or not, can be immature at times? It is not something to be held against us forever, especially if our immature defenses are not a constant pattern of dealing with the world. They are signs of the fact that we all retain some capacity for childish behavior. If, however, these are more than occasional lapses in an otherwise good adjustment, they demand more attention. We ought to do something about understanding why we employ these defenses, with an eye toward growing out of them and getting the psychological help to do it.

Understanding something about immature defense also enables us to understand other persons better. It helps us appreciate why just telling them to pull themselves together or to grow up hardly ever works. When the defenses constitute a clear pattern—when others use them habitually—they are telling us about the inner, unconscious problems with which they cannot deal directly. Defenses are informative, and when we can interpret them more clearly, we have a much better sense of what we are dealing with.

The behavior that we discount may, in fact, represent something—in a relative, a student, or a colleague—that needs more attention than we may first think. One need not be desperate to do good to read the signs of persistent immaturity correctly. We may be able to assist the person in getting the help he or she truly needs, and it is a good day whenever we can do this. We can also save ourselves from mounting frustration when we find that persons are consistently immature in their dealings with us. Once we know they are still children, we will not expect them to be adults and we will not give them adult responsibilities. We won't be so disappointed when they are so unfortunately undeveloped in their behavior and attitudes. In the next section we will explore the mature defenses. This, of course, is where we will all recognize ourselves.

Defenses: these will do quite nicely

When last we left Everyman—known now as Everyperson—he or she was struggling across the plains of the human condition weighted down with the cumbersome defenses of immaturity. Lots of us have been known to use these modes of adjustment. They work, after all, the way an unoiled suit of armor works— our protection is complete but our gracefulness of movement is diminished. Nobody gets through life without some defenses, and some are better than others, and their use reflects a mature mode of dealing with the conflicts of life. A review of the better defenses allows us to take an inventory of our own way of getting along. Perhaps we can sort through some of the less effective defenses the way we sort through the contents of a desk or kitchen drawer, always with one eye on what we may be able to throw out. The more mature defenses provide us with new and more effective styles of setting our lives in order.

Altruism has a somewhat stuffy sound but a sensible meaning. We serve ourselves well by serving others. Service is a mode of existence not without its gratifications, vicarious though these may be. Adjusting in a healthy way through serving others is not the same thing as giving up everything, saving nothing for the self, and playing out the role of the martyr. That is hurtful to the self, and in the long run a bad way of barely surviving. And there is little thanks for it. But a balanced service of others, a dedication that understands itself even as it reaches out to others—this is life that grows richer as it empties itself.

Altruism must be an aspect of all true charity, the solid base for religious or any other dedicated life.

Closely related to this is **sublimation,** which is generally defined as a mode of adjustment through which we turn the energies of certain drives away from their usual goals and toward other, more highly valued purposes. The nature and strength of the original drive are not dammed up or twisted, as in neurotic defenses, but expressed more clearly; the feelings are acknowledged, changed somewhat, and turned toward another goal. Thus, aggressive impulses may be sublimated in sports or other games, and it has been suggested that sexual drives can be turned toward many other activities, from the service of others to creativity in art. While there is some dispute about the latter formulations, there is little disagreement about the possibility of rechanneling our impulses, thus gratifying them to some extent, by doing something constructive rather than destructive with them.

Suppression is another defense that sounds grim and constricted. It has proved, however, highly useful in leading a mature life. It involves putting aside some impulse or conflict in order to deal with it later in order to keep it from interfering with our achieving the goals of the present. This is not a defense that denies the presence or the nature of the impulse. The person who uses it knows, at least on the edge of consciousness, what he or she is doing. He or she postpones dealing with the problem in order to get through the situation with which they are immediately concerned. This particular defense depends on a capacity to delay gratification—a willingness to wait for a happy ending or for a proper reward—and fails in those, and how many there are, who have not learned to do this.

Rose Kennedy in her autobiography tells of her lifelong rule never to break bad news in the evening. She actively used suppression in a sensible manner, keeping the conflicts in view but at a distance, and saving the night's sleep for her husband and other members of the family. It takes some character to use this defense, especially at a time in which we are encouraged to blab our least complaint fulsomely to anyone within earshot. But character is also the achievement of such a way of living. In a recent follow-up study on the effectiveness of defenses by psychiatrist George Valliant, suppression was used consistently by a number of the most mature subjects in his investigation. There is a trick here. It is not easy to employ this defense; it demands perspective on life and discipline of the self, commodities that seem almost from another time. It can only be used by persons who have learned to say no to themselves, at least in the short run. A healthy life is not without its deaths, the willingness to delay dealing with our conflicts, to put our feelings in the wings for a while so that we can deal with what is at the center of the stage.

This may be second cousin to *asceticism,* which is recognized by modern psychology as a mature way of handling the stress of existence. This defense builds on a sense of moral gradations between the possible choices before an individual. We can, in other words, renounce certain pleasures in order to prepare ourselves for other activities. Athletes do it in training for the various tests of their strength, and religious persons have done it for centuries for the achievement of their own spiritual goals.

People have some sense of the fittingness of this conscious denial to themselves of pleasure; asceticism is incorporated into the seasons of a mature life. We are still slogging our way through a so-called Dionysian age in which asceticism has been the slimmest shadow of an exile. And yet it remains a manner of handling existence that is not part of madness but a proved means of consolidating ourselves for better purposes. It may be that the widespread confusion about values—the crisis that has given rise to the varied searches for "value clarification"—is the inheritance of a generation that has forgotten the human need for asceticism.

Asceticism is a way of validating our sense of values, the consequence of choices about the persons and events that are of importance to us. Asceticism—even in small things—makes us look clearly at life in order to put our values in order. It may also be the only way in which we have even a small share in laying down our lives for our friends. Healthy asceticism—and it may be found more often and less self-consciously in the lives of spouses and parents than in those of the dwellers in monasteries —flows from love.

Anticipation is also a defense used by mature persons. This doesn't mean the breathless state of expectation that can define a species of anticipation. It refers rather to our ability to rehearse our reactions to difficult coming events so that we can plan for future discomfort. People who will not think about disagreeable possibilities can only be surprised and sometimes overwhelmed by them. If, however, we can feel our way into the hard times ahead, we will not be total strangers to our own reactions when they do finally occur.

This has been demonstrated in research on surgical patients: Those who secured some information about how they could expect to feel after their operations fared much better in the recovery period than those patients who stonewalled the situation emotionally. The latter were more upset, tended to blame the staff for their discomfort, and stayed longer in the hospital.

It has also been found that some measure of our grief reaction can also be anticipated, that persons can, in fact, work through some of the stages of mourning in advance and reduce the trauma of the loss of a loved one. If a spouse is terminally ill, he or she may be able to share some of the suffering in advance, making the pain easier to bear for both and giving them the powerful consolation of sharing a profound experience. This is not some smooth managing of the grimness of death, the cosmetics of psychology applied to final grief. It is rather the rediscovery of our abiding opportunities to taste life deeply by opening up rather than closing ourselves off from it.

Anticipation strengthens us for future trials; it is one of our most effective ways of dealing constructively rather than just coping with life. This is not an invitation to self-gratifying fantasy, not a stamp of approval for the daydreamer who postpones coming to grips with reality. Anticipation builds on our best human powers, on our ability to predict our future reactions based on the wisdom we have gained about our behavior in the past. We are then able to feel the future in advance and prepare ourselves so that we can retain our sense of presence even in the most trying of circumstances. People who say of distressing possibilities, "I don't want to think about that," do themselves a disservice and actually make themselves more vulnerable than they need be. Anticipation does not demand excessive self-dramatization; its strength flows from its realism. The same principle that lies beneath fire drills and disaster plans also works well in our personal lives.

The saving grace of *humor* remains a prize within the reach of all but the hard of heart. Humor gets us through places where solemnity can never make a safe passage. It does so by allowing us to express our feelings without hurting ourselves or others; it saves us from paralysis in the face of life's conflicts. I once read in a textbook that humor "allows one to bear and yet focus on what is too terrible to be borne." Such humor is redemptive for all of us weighed down with difficulties that pass through different stages rather than get solved; with unfairness the rule in the distribution of good looks, physical grace, and intelligence; with things waiting to go wrong at the sound of our approaching footfall; with no adequate splint available for a universe chronically out of joint. Humor allows us to laugh with forgiveness at ourselves and our dilemmas—a lavish blessing from our maker.

Humor, of course, must be distinguished from *wit*, which is not nearly so constructive or useful to us in life. Wit, which can be as biting as a polar wind, fails to redeem because it distracts us from what we are feeling. It does not help us to bear it; it can only make us look away from it. Humor is a mature defense, but wit is a weapon, and we can damage ourselves and others with it. Wit may be the chief means of protection for the cynic, for the distant persons who don't want anyone too close to them. Such wit, unflavored by irony or compassion, can wound but it cannot heal. You can tell the difference immediately between gentle humor and savage wit. One gets us through the worst of things, while the other makes our pilgrimage darker and more lonely.

Healing through forgiveness

Reconciliation, forgiveness, amnesty—these words ring like bells in the consciousness of this decade. They are notions to lift the soul, and yet any discussion is often bitter to the taste. Some people demand that we grant them amnesty without hesitation; others draw plans for reconciling us, on their terms, of course, whether we are ready for reconciliation or not. These are great subjects to make speeches about, but how do we deal sensibly and sensitively with them in everyday life?

There are some things we understand about all important human transactions; just as they hold true for trusting and loving, so, too, they characterize forgiveness. First of all, we experience such things with our whole selves if we are to experience them at all. Nothing works when it comes only from one aspect of our personalities. Just thinking or just feeling are not enough in themselves. We must both understand the situation and acknowledge the meaning of our emotions so that we can be as fully present in forgiveness as possible.

Forgiveness, like love, demands that we *be there*, that we establish contact, that we touch each other's depths, that we make a difference to, rather than just a checkmark about, each other. This sounds complicated and in a way it is, but we all know when we do it and when we fail to. And we also know what it takes from ourselves to be with others in a personal way. So we start out knowing more than we thought.

Second, and again like anything else that is truly human, we will never forgive perfectly. Forgive with our full persons, yes, and from the heart as well, but we will always fall short of perfection in the matter. That's okay, of course, because so powerful is the strength of forgiveness that it works even in a diluted solution. Everything we do that makes any difference in life works exactly the same way.

We get over some things, we get better at others, but we never get the richest of our human experiences down cold. We are a race of imperfect individuals who can nevertheless get into, enlarge, strengthen, and heal each other. We help pay off each other's spiritual mortgages all the time; this is what we all do in leading purposeful and sensitive lives. What else can we do for each other anyway?

Forgiveness is a basic attitude necessary for being able to live with each other at all. Forgiving is part of the daily existence of persons who live close enough to rub each other the wrong way now and then. It is also encouraging to realize that forgiveness works even when we get it only half right. Indeed, that is why the generous impulse to forgive invites the other closer to us; we are ready to meet, as the old saying goes, halfway. But that is the longest part of the journey.

Third, it takes time for these processes to work. Nothing that lasts is ever put together in a mere few hours or over a weekend —not even that old favorite, love at first sight. That, as we know, is only a beginning and so, too, is the moment of opening our heart in forgiveness. Humanly, however, we live and move in and through time or we don't get very far at all. Forgiveness builds on patience, and it works out its meaning and effects slowly but surely.

And, last, forgiveness begins at home. If we can forgive ourselves we find it much easier to absolve others. But some of us deny ourselves forgiveness, refusing to accept ourselves or standing back in the shadows of shame and regret because we are sometimes so much less than we would like to be. This is a way of punishing ourselves, of course, of giving ourselves what we deserve for being so filled with guilt. However, it is a harsh way to deal with oneself; it is like locking yourself in a room without windows where you can only get sick of yourself.

Forgiveness unlocks that door and throws open the windows; it frees us for life once more. The biggest step we take out of ourselves is the one we make when we can face our failings clearly, identify them accurately, and still agree to live with ourselves. In many ways this is the beginning of everything that is significant in life, because it puts us in touch with who we really are.

The many sides of forgiveness

In *Hope for the Flowers* (Newman Press, 1972), one of the storied caterpillars, caught in a throng of fellow creatures climbing up a pillar, asks the question, "How can I step on someone I've just talked to?" Maybe a veteran subway rider would be able to handle that question easily; in fact, mass transit riders frequently end up stepping on and talking to other people at the same time. For most of us, however, the question is better phrased in another way: "How can I talk to someone I've just stepped on?"

Learning how to forgive and to allow oneself to be forgiven are two of the hardest and most important parts of life. It may be easy to love one's enemies in the abstract but it is very hard to forgive them face to face. The problem may be found in its most serious form when we must face and forgive our friends or our family, the people with whom we most regularly exchange hurts.

Sometimes the situations in which we step on others are those we would rather file and forget, pretending either that they never happened or that we did not mean them in quite the way they came out. We may be tempted to do that or, on the other hand, we can overreact to overcome the guilt or shame we feel at what we may have said or done. Neither of these attitudes deals straightforwardly with the occasions, many of them minor, on which we wound or are wounded by other persons. Turning away from it does not make the situation go away and overreacting may be aimed at clearing up our own feelings rather than healing those of the offended person. It takes a steady eye and a firm heart to come to terms with ourselves and the issues that are involved in the challenges of forgiveness.

What do I mean when I say I'm sorry?   That is a phrase that can be uttered in a quite perfunctory manner, much in the way a train conductor punches a ticket, and with a similar intention. It is a way of securing passage rather than a way of reestablishing relationship. When "I'm sorry" is said in an impersonal tone, it does not really deliver the transforming message of human forgiveness. These words always depend on how much of ourselves we put into them. There is no magic unless we are there. That is a traditional challenge, of course, and it applies to any of the important statements we exchange with each other. Hurt is transmitted personally; likewise, forgiveness must be communicated with as much of ourselves as possible involved in the exchange.

We never know what hurts people.   Perhaps the worst emotional wounds we inflict are those of which we are least aware. Concentrating on ourselves and our own concerns, the rights and needs of others can become obscured in our own eyes so that we hardly notice when we step on them. Sometimes people are hurt without sufficient cause; sometimes they lead with their chins so that they cannot help but be hurt. In many circumstances, however, a hurt comes because of a blunder on our part, a failure to take the other person's feelings or interests into account. Perhaps if we think of some of the small things that hurt us, we will become more sensitized to our own capacity to hurt others without even recognizing it.

Much forgiveness is symbolic.   The rituals of absolution and forgiveness—those gestures through which we make a relationship whole again—are powerfully important and cannot be disregarded. They are part of our human language and, as a people, we are poorer when we let them fall into disuse for whatever reason. This is a particular danger in an era in which remaining cool has been exalted as the height of human behavior. Those who prize coolness will never be able to express forgiveness symbolically because they must give too much of themselves away in the process. They cannot easily say *I love you,* and they will only be surprised when loneliness finally catches up with them.

Just as we must learn to use the language of symbols, so, too, we must be able to understand it. Sometimes the best another person can do is make a small gesture that has a large meaning in our regard; a widow's mite of a symbol but still the best the other can possibly do in a given situation. To reject it or to ignore it—to demand unconditional surrender on our terms— may make us feel self-righteous, but it can also be a very hollow victory. Read the small gestures that seek forgiveness correctly and your life will be enlarged, as will those of the persons who make such gestures to you.

Forgiveness is like time for our attention.   Forgiveness, after all, is one of the few things we can give to other people freely. It is also something that can neither be purchased nor demanded, and its only service is in other persons. Forgiveness, in fact, can only be given away. If we make other people pay for it or if we use it as a psychological weapon associated with emotional manipulation rather than genuine change of heart, it fails. Forgiveness is something precious because through it we can make each other new once more and open each other to the freshness of life again. Sometimes genuine forgiveness is so powerful that others refuse it, simply because they know that they will have to change in order to accept such a loving gift. This does not make us abandon our efforts to forgive or to seek forgiveness, but it does alert us to the fact that this is a precious human commodity that can make the difference between life and death both for us and for those who live closely with us.

Rules to remember

Things go wrong all the time: There is absolutely no exception to this rule. You can apply it in any place or in any set of circumstances. No matter how much preparation has been made, no matter how many countdowns or checklists have been run through, most things tend to go wrong. This happens in families, business, and even in that antiseptic and supposedly feelingless world of mathematics in which ill-fed computers regularly frustrate the most scientifically pure hearts. That things regularly go wrong is a basic truism of the human condition. Our trouble arises when we are unrealistically optimistic, still hoping for perfection when experience tells us that we should know better.

If things did not systematically go wrong, at least in small details, we would never have crabgrass, lovers' quarrels, or disappointments. We would never need love; nor would we ever have the chance to experience the kind of growth that takes place in us when we approach each other with genuine forgiveness. Part of what goes wrong, you see, is us; we are still capable of betraying our own best intentions or resolutions and of not knowing quite why we do these things. We may never figure out quite why, or plumb the depths of our psychological motivations completely. This is why it is vital for forgiveness to be at hand, both for us to receive and for us to give away.

Good people get to understand and to tolerate us: It is amazing, in fact, how, with real affection, our family and friends get to know and to forgive us for being the imperfect specimens we are. Life would be absolutely intolerable if this loving capacity were not present in those around us. This is something good people do without thinking about it very much, a reaction compounded of healthy instincts and openness.

It goes beyond just putting up with us, as a matter of fact, because it includes a kind of patient acceptance that tells us in effect, "We understand and care for you even when you are very difficult to get along with." Families probably would not survive if they could not create this buffer zone around the temperamental, the distraught, or the just plain ornery members of the group. It is a zone of blessing in which others suspend judgment while the offending member has time to come to terms with and reintegrate himself or herself with the group. This is done silently and symbolically most of the time and it is a sure cure for sulking, feeling sorry for oneself, or the other hazards that are involved in growing up or in remaining grown up.

A sense of humor helps: It always does, of course, but perhaps in no situation is it more important than in that of forgiveness. We cannot stand on a pedestal of distorted self-regard if we really care about forgiving and being forgiven by others. We cannot remain on a lofty platform and maintain our illusions about ourselves when forgiveness demands, first of all, a sense of realism about both our limitations and our possibilities. We need not ridicule ourselves in order to be able to laugh in a healthy manner at our own foibles and shortcomings. Nothing clears the head of vanity better than a general and smiling confrontation with our own fumbling selves. When we can accept the cracks in our own character structure without being unnecessarily mad at ourselves because they are there in the first place, we are far more able to accept those we will always find in others.

Self-treatment

If we begin by trying to forgive ourselves for our failures, our mistaken judgments, or our overestimations of our own powers, we take a big step toward being able to give that same forgiveness to other persons. There is no substitute, in other words, for facing the truth about ourselves. It helps to have that sense of humor we just mentioned, but only if we use it as a gentle light that enables us to acknowledge more of ourselves. We cannot laugh off the wrongs we have committed if we are going to talk to those we have just stepped on; we begin by facing the true dimensions of what we have done. That is not an easy task, but there can be no forgiveness from ourselves or from others if we do not put an honest name to the injury we have caused. And that's just the beginning. The following are also important:

Don't nurse the hurt: This applies in those situations in which we feel that we have been wrongly treated by someone else. One of our most familiar human temptations is to hold on to hurts that we should learn to let go of. It is far better to get our injury exposed to the air than to let it fester in angry brooding through which we isolate ourselves and make ourselves more miserable than the human condition really demands. It is understandable that we want to nurse our wounds, because at times there doesn't seem to be anything else we can do about them. We can, however, at least admit that we are doing this and try to accept our wounded selves with the kind of forgiveness we are not quite ready to give to others.

Forgive others as you would have them forgive you.   This is one of the better translations of the Golden Rule or of the scriptural instruction that we must love our enemies. If we try to offer forgiveness as we would like to receive it, we will necessarily begin to try to see into the world of the other person. Seeing something of another person's viewpoint almost always improves our own way of looking at things. We become more tolerant, and through understanding, we heal far more wounds than we do by argumentation about who said what or for what reasons. Disputing how the fight got started in the first place only makes things worse, and it is exhausting besides.

Hurt collectors

A famous psychiatrist once described a certain class of persons as "injustice collectors," people who make a lifestyle out of being offended. There are no real reasons for their being offended, of course, so they invent them, reading into the behavior of others in fanciful ways so that they can finally accumulate enough evidence to accuse them of imaginary hurts. This is a strange way to relate to other people, a sad and diminished way to live in general, and there are two reasons it is very difficult to deal with forgiveness with these people.

First of all, they have not really been hurt, and second, they don't want anything to do with forgiveness. They get through life in this unhealthy fashion, offering friendship to others as bait for a trap they finally close when the other least understands or expects it.

It is good to remember that these people are really telling us more about their own troubles than they are about anything else. Most good people do not want to offend others, and they are taken aback when they seem to be accused by one of these "hurt collectors." They should not lose confidence in themselves but try to see this as part of the pattern of the other's behavior; they should neither be dismayed nor manipulated by the offended attitude of the other. That is playing the game according to his rules, which is just what he wants you to do. It is better to be acceptant and understanding—and to restrain oneself from trying to straighten the situation out rationally. The meaning of the problem is emotional and it cannot be described or treated by intellectual means. We can, however, realize that if we could look deeply enough into their life histories, we would understand them better and know why they have forged such a sad and shabby way of getting on with others. In short; understanding, yes; involvement, no.

Being sensitive

A man or a woman pays a high price for being sensitive, for feeling all the aspects of what occurs in his or her own experience, or for sensing and caring about even those tragedies that do not touch their own lives directly. It hurts to pay attention to life and to look at its cruelties and injustices, its small deceits and its big disappointments, and to try to keep faith with it rather than to turn cynical. It is difficult to see other people as persons rather than members of a crowd or a mob, and it is genuinely hard to remember that each individual has feelings and meanings all his or her own that must be appreciated and respected by others. Sometimes life just seems to hurt too much to look squarely at it, and yet if we give up on this, we blunt ourselves to the meaning of our existence and, in the name of missing some of its sorrows, we deprive ourselves of any feelings for its joys. Only the person who is open to life in its bad parts as well as its good can possess the kind of happiness that is the special prize of the open heart.

This sensitivity to the feelings of others also allows you to be honest about yourself and your own life experience. Best of all, even the reverberating echoes of our own hurts tell us that we have touched life and meaning, that we have not stayed on the sidelines and that we have not run away out of fear. Perhaps the contemporary meaning of "turning the other cheek" involves us in opening ourselves to the pain of the whole world and in not shrugging it off or in trying to distract ourselves from it. It is better to be alive with this kind of feeling for mankind than to be dead to it, because we have become estranged from compassion for our fellow pilgrims. Those who mourn are those who are comforted, and those who can share the world's pain are those who finally triumph over it.

CHAPTER 6

A time to weep and a time to laugh
A time to mourn and a time to
dance . . .

Who owns joy?

Joy is supposedly the possession of believers, but even we have been very grim lately. A lot of solemnity—like the flu—has been going around. Perhaps this is because the values and virtues that underlie joy have received so much ridicule. These are simple things like honesty and fidelity. You can never experience joy without these; yet honesty is hard to find and fidelity is thought to be more relic than reality in the modern world.

There is more to joy than laughter, of course, but the capacity to laugh in a healthy manner is indeed one of the sounds of operative joy. Laughter comes in various forms; there is bitter laughter, the skulking and soundless laughter that goes with a smirk, and the hostile laughter of ridicule. Worst of all, perhaps, is canned laughter, that collection of ghostly automatic echoes that is not laughter at all. Laughter is too precious to be wasted in these ways.

It takes a special realism about oneself to be able to laugh from the heart. That is very different from the hard-forced laughter of hangers-on and yes-men. Different too from the "loud laugh" that Oliver Goldsmith said spoke of "the vacant mind." Laughter that is joyful belongs to persons who are honest about themselves and faithful to this truth and to each other. Laughter is a special prize of the joyful, whose solid values are the treasure that cannot be consumed by rust or destroyed by moths.

And more besides

Joy goes along with a special vision of things, a vision to be shared rather than clutched to one's breast. It has no relationship to the self-righteousness and smug piety that have taken so much joy out of religion. Joy does not exist in persons who are afraid of losing themselves; in fact, it shines in the lives of persons who gladly spend themselves and their energies in the service of others in a free and loving way. Joy may be best understood by inspecting its correlates. These include:

Believing. No one who is cynical can ever be joyful. You cannot sneer at the world and give up on it or write it off as crooked and fixed in every way. Joy is the inheritance of those who continue to commit themselves to others even after they have been hurt or disappointed. The unhappiest of people are those who stop believing; that is equivalent to committing suicide of the spirit, a survival without a taste for living.

Struggling. Joy would have no meaning in an environment totally free of struggle, in a place where there is nothing to do, no hopes to realize, no hurts to be healed, no gifts of the self to be given. All this means is that joy coexists with life. As a French author once put it, "One inch of joy surmounts of grief a span / because to laugh is proper to the man."

Enjoyment. This signifies our ability to take delight in life and in each other as well as the world all around us. Enjoyment can only be appreciated by persons who are open to the world, who take the time to look at it and to discover what is good about it. The same attitude exists between friends who find a very special kind of joy because they are able to look at the world together.

Involvement. Over the last several years involvement has gotten a bad name. It conjures, in the way the Puritan world once did, a vision of grimness in pursuit of right and virtue. It hardly makes us think of smiling faces, happy people, or joyful sounds. And yet the most involved people I know, like the priests in Belfast, are not grim at all. Genuine involvement denotes seriousness of purpose, but it also implies a profoundly human grasp on life. Seriousness and grimness are not synonymous, and individuals who are most involved in life are not strangers to laughter and joy. It is serious, for example, to march with Cesar Chavez and the members of the United Farm Workers. You cannot, however, be with them long without discovering that they are filled with joy; gentle laughter is as much their symbol as the black eagle on their banners.

Compassion.   Joy goes along with a feeling for the world of persons and their struggles. It indicates that we can appreciate the nobility of persons and yet recognize their foibles and absurdities as well. This special vision is a warmhearted capacity to accept and forgive all of us who belong to the same flawed yet wondrous family. An itch to judge and condemn, a passion for vengeance that is untempered—these feelings ordinarily put joy to death very swiftly.

What is joy?

Joy is not mindless.   It is not some silliness, giggles arising from adolescent uneasiness or from some desperate search for distraction and pleasure. Joy comes from an ability to enter into life in depth, and the laughter to which it gives birth is not shallow or cold. Joy, in one of the abiding paradoxes, belongs more easily to those who accept the scars of life than it does to those who try to avoid them.

Joy is something to share, one of those remarkable gifts that we can never lose once we truly possess it. Not only can we give it away, we want to give it away. In some fashion we cannot help but give it away. It multiplies rather than diminishes by this action of sharing. Joy is not a possession we have to worry about or hoard; joy flourishes with an openhanded and loving attitude toward life.

Joy is a religious event.   We only understand the truly religious aspects of our experience through knowing and loving people. Religious teachings remain only theoretical unless they can be translated into human terms. Joy is one of the most important of these. We can wound, but we can also heal. We can damage a relationship with each other and yet, by honestly facing our own shortcomings, we can meet on new and higher ground, having deepened our love rather than destroyed it. We can give life to the discouraged and hope to those who seem ready to give up. This prepares us to face death confidently; the joyful know death cannot have dominion over them.

Laughing at ourselves

One of the best therapies known to the human race is our ability to laugh at ourselves. This should be compassionate, forgiving laughter, the kind that redeems us from the corners into which we paint ourselves, the joyous laughter that goes with sunshine and love. Sir Max Beerbohm once wrote that "nobody ever died of laughter," but we might add that many people have been cured by it. It takes a special angle of vision to be able to view our inconsistencies and forgive ourselves for them at the same time, to recognize what is funny about us and to keep real faith with ourselves anyway. To laugh at oneself requires some distance, a kind of perspective that puts things back into proportion again. It is particularly important to laugh at ourselves on a regular basis; it is only when we take ourselves too seriously that we forget who we are or misplace our identity. We need laughter to get through life, and it may help to review periodically the situations in which our humorous but touching side can be appreciated.

We look funny, for example, sneaking glances at ourselves in store windows or mirrors to check our appearance; we look funny when we try to look either younger or older than we are. We are almost hilarious in those moments when we think we are wise enough to tell other people how to live; even better at those times when we are trying to look as though we took the advice of others seriously. We are amusing when, at parties, we look as if we are animated members of one group while we are really trying to hear what is going on in the group next to us. Make your own list in the quiet of the night and have it ready whenever you feel a case of solemnity coming on.

Living with pain

What is the obvious question to ask a healthy man who is in his nineties? The late book editor Hiram Hayden put the question we all care about to just such a person, a poet and lawyer named Melville Crane. What, Mr. Hayden wanted to know, was the secret of Crane's longevity. When Crane was certain that the question was a serious one, he paused and answered, "I have learned to live with pain," and quickly went on to another subject.

Most of us are looking for a different answer to help us find our way into a long life. We would like to hear about some diet, some schedule, even some favorite prayer, guaranteed to bring lasting good health. And yet this old man's answer is better than most of the promises we get about the wonderful results of certain vitamins or exercises. And we all want the secret to be painless and quick. But it takes a long time to learn to live with pain and, though we may look in many a good book, we won't find anything better to help us grow in either wisdom or holiness.

What kind of pain?

There are pains that are easy to characterize and others that even the poets don't seem to have the words to describe fully. Living with pain does not, however, mean just getting along when we have a toothache, although this is something with which we do have to learn to live. Coping, we call it these days, and it means maintaining some balance in a world that seems bent on knocking us down with the small pressures of flat tires, missed appointments, and rainy days.

The pain we have to manage day by day over the long haul is the kind that goes with serious living. To take our existence seriously and to involve ourselves in it purposefully brings peace and joy, but we pass through pain to reach these. Even though we may be surrounded by friends and fame, we cannot escape this special kind of suffering because it goes with being alive. This pain may never exactly become a friend, but we get to know and recognize it as not necessarily an enemy, either. It goes with discovering the good things, the lasting things in life, like fidelity and love, and when we accept it, we find peace as well.

How do we do it?

We live with this pain not by denying it in some stoical fashion, pretending that it does not hurt and working hard to fool other people into thinking that it doesn't bother us. Nor do we live with it by fighting it, the way an ill-matched husband and wife sometimes battle their way stressfully through a marriage. Living with our pain is possible when we understand something of its inevitability and grasp something of its rhythm and ultimate meaning in our lives. We can then make some room for it because we understand that it is part of the cost of living a life that has genuine significance.

There is no point in kicking against the goad or in struggling needlessly with the pain that is almost a seam in the human condition. Fighting it or trying to drown it out just makes things worse for us in the long run. If we can learn not to make things in life worse than they are, we take a big step toward learning how to live peacefully with pain.

Living with something is far different from battling it to a draw. It builds on our understanding of the characteristics of that with which we live. And that can be a person, a handicap, or a talent. We have to respect these things and not try to change them unnecessarily. We make peace with things like pain by understanding it more deeply and by gradually seeing its relationship to the overall pattern of life. Some pain is involved with everything that is worthwhile.

It is, for example, seeded deep into love and work, and it does not necessarily dominate these experiences. It resembles a lesser motif in a symphony—something always present but integrally related to the overall composition. We are not masochists when we recognize that everything that is valuable, everything that demands our full presence, possesses some dimension of suffering. Wherever life is found, there are small deaths to be faced each day. Such suffering or death never constitute the end for persons of faith, however, because they understand that these are necessary conditions of life.

Pain is part of honest living, true loving, and real believing. We learn to live with it by committing ourselves not to the pain but to the activities of which it is only a part. We love for better reasons than to suffer; but we accept the suffering in love for these same good reasons. We cannot love without letting go of something; we give ourselves up all the time in trying to reach others in genuine love. But we experience a fullness at the same time. We have yielded up something of ourselves yet, by the same action, made room in our lives for others.

Special kinds of pain

There are many pains other than those of love, of course, that we must face. We manufacture many of them ourselves. They arise ordinarily because we are not able to accept who we are. We have overrated the easiness of accepting our true selves. It only sounds easy. It is a lifelong process through which we have to face ourselves honestly over and over again. The pain of always facing the truth is far less than the pains that come when we possess a distorted notion of ourselves. This is the kind of pain that we can do something about. But while it lasts, the pain associated with a false perception of ourselves is a killer indeed. This pain takes our life away because it causes us to defend ourselves against the truth. It chokes us by denying us the fresh air of our own authenticity. Psychological defenses used in extreme ways are, like cigarettes, quite dangerous for those who use them. They enable us to live with a twisted picture of ourselves, with at least minor delusions of grandeur. But this does something to us down deep that is difficult to repair.

Sometimes we shrink from the investment of ourselves that we must make if we are to live in friendship with other persons. We like to avoid those things that hold the possibility of pain for us. We move away from these things, smoothing over issues that should be faced, obscuring differences that should be recognized, letting the most important aspects of human relationships go unattended until they boil over.

We do this when we go through life trying to avoid conflicts in order to preserve ourselves from suffering. And yet the effort to avoid these difficulties becomes a tortured exercise that makes it very difficult for us to find our way through life. When we insist on roundabout paths to keep an illusion of peace and calm in our lives, we are like the deluded Chamberlain returning, in 1938, to England with a worthless Nazi promise.

An example

Family life causes pain, and some people suggest we do away with it because it is complex and imperfect and gives us so much trouble. There is a lot of suffering connected with family life, there is no question about that; and yet the notion of abandoning this institution is an oversimplified dream. The family, you see, is the only institution we know in which human beings really thrive. It is strong and tough, an evolutionary product that still meets human needs better than any of the other scenarios offered by contemporary reformers. Make people freer of this institution, they seem to promise, and there will be less suffering. But we do not escape suffering by getting out of things, and seldom by despising our traditions or institutions. They help us bear and understand our pain. We make pain worse by mindlessly destroying them.

Sometimes people can rationalize away taking responsibility because they say they want to save people pain. I recall, for example, a young man telling me recently that he hoped that his future bride would have had premarital sex relations because he did not want to take on the awesome responsibility of being the first one to love her. He made it sound fine, a cool argument for a cool age, and yet, of course, it is hard to know what he was really saying, except that he was backing away from life, perhaps to avoid some of its pain but almost certainly sentencing himself to a good deal of it at some later stage of the game. There is no way out of the pain that goes with important things. And such rationalizing doesn't help us live with pain at all. It just postpones pain and sometimes makes it much worse when it finally comes.

Forgetting pain

We can also be grateful for the blessing we share at being able to forget pain while we remember happiness. That widely recognized truth tells us something of the power and relative strength of these two common elements. Happiness survives, but pain disappears when faced with the test of time. There is comfort for us in realizing that if we seek a meaningful life, if we have a developed sense of values, we will work out a favorable balance between joy and suffering in our lives. That is the message we so often receive from people who suffer great hardship and yet smile because they have something rich and real within themselves.

We learn something from the poor in spirit, for example, who seem to know how to give everything away without losing anything in the bargain. And what of the handicapped, for whom pain is not imaginary, who manage to create and contribute to the lives of everybody around them? Persons with inner peace bring a special grace to every life they touch. How did these people get this way? We are tempted to think it must be luck, an accident of birth, or perhaps a favorable star that shone on their birth.

The answer, of course, is found in none of these notions. They have done something about life and its challenges. They have looked pain in the face and have refused to be stared down by it. Their peace did not come by accident but through a series of their own serious choices about their values and their willingness to face and deal with life straightforwardly. They give us an example that helps us regain our own lives and possess our own souls anew. Living with our pain is the condition of our pilgrimage to joy.

"Liberating" people from their grief

The best intentions sometimes bring us to the edge of our worst choices. And is there a better intention than wanting to help people who hang on the gibbet of grief? It is a holy thing to comfort those who mourn, but how do we best do it?

This question rose again recently when an extremely sincere priest asked me about techniques "to liberate" a widow from her grief. It would seem a blessing to be able to free the afflicted from the heavy, black-ribboned weight of mourning. But here, as in so many other crucial events of life, there are no techniques that can do this. Indeed, it may be our own need to do something in the face of difficult circumstances that moves us to free people from experiences they cannot humanly escape.

Our pilgrimage through life is not a parade, and it certainly is not a forced march. We count ourselves blessed if we find two or three people with whom we can keep in step along the way, but the journey itself is that of a shambling crowd, its members with different starting points and a variety of strides. And the path itself splits off; there are long and sometimes tortuous side roads that only wind slowly back to the main highway. There are places to pause and not a few dead ends. The secret of it all lies in letting people find their own way and in restraining ourselves from making them march in the direction or at the rate of our choosing. Grief is one of the passages in this journey, and it leads people for a time off the central path; they fall out of step and may be a long time making their way back. There is, however, no saving persons from these detours through grief; there is no way to take their place, no way to "liberate" them from the necessity of mourning.

Even the most caring and unselfish can do little more than give people room to do what Freud described as the "work of mourning." No cajolery, no empty reassurances, no species of denial does anything but distract them—and sometimes delay them—from getting at the work only they can do for themselves in their journey through the stages of grief. Being with people in an understanding and acceptant way, just simply being there without interfering while they carry out what sometimes seem the bizarre symbolic aspects of mourning, being present without the hurried quality of funeral home visitors eager to sign the register and be gone—through this we make purchase of comfort for those who mourn.

Such simple but powerful human presence—we can all tell when somebody is "with us" or not—creates the environment in which people can enter into the mourning they cannot escape. And only if they enter it—only if they take that path that angles off sharply from the main road of life—can they make their way through it and emerge, their grief work done, on the other side of it. People make themselves whole again through the ordeal of mourning; they come to terms with their loss and reintegrate themselves into life, joining the long pilgrimage of existence once more.

The work of grief is largely symbolic; its energies are expended at the unconscious level, and it is sometimes difficult for onlookers to make rational sense of what goes on at the surface level of consciousness. Grieving people may, for example, search for the lost person in places that were familiar settings in their life together. They may pass through numbness and into anger before they reach acceptance.

What grieving persons do may not seem to fit together unless we can grasp its symbolic meaning, unless we can sense the bereaved efforts to find and reincorporate their lost one in some way. The fact that we do not understand the process completely does not mean that we should not let it proceed at its own pace. People find their way through grief and emerge different but healed if we try to stay with them and give them time and space in which to carry out this indispensable human and profoundly religious activity. Knowing when to stand aside while remaining personally present is the great gift that cannot be called a technique. Our presence is a vessel of healing grace, the richest and surest source of comfort for those who must mourn.

Can you anticipate grief?

It is helpful, according to those who have observed the process, for persons to anticipate some aspects of mourning. For example, a married couple may find this a rich and healing experience, even if they can only share a small portion of anticipated grief, when one of them is suffering a terminal illness. A death-denying society, however, still emphasizes denial, so that great debates rage about telling patients exactly how sick they are, and the very sound of the word *death* is softened by a dozen cushioned synonyms. This is why playwright Robert Anderson a few years ago told a conference on death of his own deep regrets at not telling his wife of the seriousness of her illness. He felt that he had missed an opportunity to share what, as it turned out, they both bore in separate anguish: the reality of her impending death. Here again, those who wish to comfort are wise enough not to force people into discussing death and tasting the first stages of grief before they themselves are ready for it. But we can support them in their moments of choice about this and be with them at the times when they may be strong enough to let themselves be weak by putting aside denial in order to face the truth together.

A day when you don't get anything done

These kinds of days happen to everybody. Just check your experience if you have any doubt. Recall the days when you have had your work planned out very carefully. This may even have depended on setting a day aside, leaving it open for this particular task and feeling good about the prospect of finishing a project. And then shortly after dawn the day begins to unravel. First, only a thread or two, but then they spin free, dervishlike, until we are knee-deep in the shredded fabric of what should have been a good day.

First of all there is the telephone, which may have been silent for weeks. Now it rings as though your office were headquarters in a national emergency. And, of course, unexpected things do occur, emergencies of a sort, that require your attention either in your office, school, or back at home. These are not discrete little emergencies; they are long, continuing emergencies that string themselves across the hours of the day like lines across prairie telephone poles.

Add in a few misunderstandings with the kind of people you really don't want to have misunderstandings with in the first place. You know the kind of misunderstanding: You want to clear it up, and the more you try the worse it gets and so the more distracted you are as you try to turn back to your own work. Unexpected bills arrive, and there is usually a mistake in your bank statement thrown in for good measure. Things and people seem to be breaking down all around you. And all the while frustration mounts. The sun is now high in the sky, the clock is ticking relentlessly away, and you are behind the line of scrimmage, your work untouched and your spirits in disarray.

A danger for obsessives . . .

This is a particularly trying problem for obsessives. It gets them where it hurts them most—in their schedule. They can handle a lot of things, but disrupting a long-planned program of activity is disconcerting. The anguish of obsessives increases geometrically as the delays increase arithmetically. Obsessives go to bed happy when they get things done, in good order, and in good time. These days make that impossible and offer no comfort in return. The interrupted day is generally followed by a restless night.

To be distinguished from . . .

The days when we don't get anything done are, of course, to be distinguished from days on which we don't do much of anything. There is a radical difference. It is possible, even on occasion for obsessives, to arrange distractions so that they never get at the work that is piled up on their desks. It is a form of avoidance behavior. They find little things to do that mount up, multiply, and seem to fill the earth. They have to sharpen their pencils, find just the right kind of typewriter paper, check the mail, make a few phone calls, and the day dies at their own hands.

They may not want to admit it—although they have a sneaking suspicion that they are the guilty persons—but they get something out of not getting at the work. Some people spend their entire lives finding small jobs to do so that they can keep a safe distance from the large ones that they should do. This is not the kind of problem we are talking about. It is related, however, and is worth our meditation.

Things to learn

There may be many things to learn on such occasions. We have all ended up with the last sand of the day trickling through our fingers, realizing that not much was accomplished. What do these days tell us, even those of us who think we know ourselves pretty well? Is there a Providence suddenly embracing our calendar, trying to teach us something? Is it better to learn or to burn (with frustration, of course)?

Such days help us understand ourselves even better than participating in an encounter group could. We stand revealed on the occasions when our plans go awry. We not only see more clearly how well we cope with sudden inconveniences but we also learn something more about our style and things we care about.

What values, for example, are most important when we find ourselves in conflict? What are the things that we try at all costs to get done when the pressure is on us? And are these things we get done mostly for our own satisfaction or are they things that are ordered truly to the service or enlightenment of others? We may discover that on such days we put a high priority on satisfying our own needs. That may be one of the reasons the interruption of such days is so disconcerting for us. We may be thrown off more than usual because we find it so difficult to move away from our own concerns and to respond freely to the needs of others. It isn't that we don't want to help others. It may just be that over the years we develop a style in which our schedule and our program is so inviolate that we lose some of our freedom to understand and respond to those around us. Perhaps our concentration on our own aims—or our slowly developed obsessiveness—focuses us too narrowly on ourselves, and we only discover it when our schedule is interrupted.

In perspective . . .

After all, what we experience rarely on such an interrupted day may be a commonplace experience for many other persons, especially parents who find this is the normal condition of family life. Learning to cope with change, with the constantly shifting needs of others, without losing themselves in the process is a special part of the vocation of parenthood that demands that a mother and father stay in relationship to their children even when the children are shifting so fast that the parents don't quite seem to understand them anymore. This, of course, is one of the richest meanings of love; it asks us to put aside our plans when the legitimate needs of others present themselves to us. This is not the same as the I-must-save-the-world syndrome of the do-gooders. It is closer to a core of loving that demands we let our own wishes die and that we feel the painful price of this sacrifice. We give up a rigid neatness of life as we get better at loving others.

The most important things of all

It is never a bad day if we manage to do what is important. It may be that on the days we don't seem to get anything done, in reality, we are doing the most important things of all. For on these days we have the opportunity to experience life a little more deeply precisely because it is not seamlessly perfect and under control like so many of our other days. Perhaps we learn that life cannot really be controlled, not if it's going to be a deeply human and productive life anyway, a free-standing existence neither insulated against nor alienated from spontaneity.

Maybe on such days we learn a little bit more about letting go, one of life's hardest but most necessary lessons. We cannot live very happily or very deeply unless we face the mystery of letting go of things and persons. We must let go of what we so desperately clutch and move with events without unnecessarily mourning the things that are past or wringing our hands over what we must let go or leave behind if we are to make our way into the future. This is a lesson in frustrating days that extends to all seasons. If we cannot clutch to our own schedules, we learn that we cannot clutch too possessively to people when they must go their own ways. And we may learn something about facing the surrenders of self that are implicit in illness, retirement, and even death.

Thanksgiving, not regrets

So regrets are not the only way to handle the days when we seem constantly to be interrupted. We are on the edge of mystery whenever our adjustment is disrupted because, if we look, we can suddenly see more deeply into ourselves and into the swift-moving currents of life around us. We need not seek these days out, providing distractions too readily for ourselves, but we can be ready to meet them without feeling that we are losing everything in the process. Indeed, if we can enter into these days, we may gain far more than we suspect. Balance is the thing, of course, but maintaining our balance may be one of the best lessons we learn on the days when we can't seem to get anything done. We can thank God for such surprises, because they are part of his gift of life to us, a surprising and unpredictable set of blessings that give us growth by always asking more of us.

CHAPTER 7

A time to scatter stones and a time to gather them A time to embrace and a time to be far from embraces . . .

Let's be reasonable

People say this all the time. And it does sound good. It is a noble and profoundly human phrase, built on what we consider to be our most distinguishing characteristic. The only trouble is that the world does not run that way. Most of the time when people use the phrase, they mean just the opposite. There is just no way in which they are going to be reasonable.

Think, for example, of the late Lyndon Johnson, when, putting his arm around some adversary's shoulder, he would quote the Bible, "Come, let us reason together." Those words came across to many with all the unreason of an old-fashioned dentist planting one foot on your chest to get better leverage to yank out a tooth while saying, "This won't hurt you a bit." Former President Johnson, it is said, was signaling not a moment for a logical exchange but instead was making a clearing in which he could manipulate, jawbone, or just finally wear down any opposition. It was a sign that he was about to use the force of emotion more than rules of logic. So it is with most of us.

Our lack of reason is something that we recognize, but, as with many serious things, we sometimes talk about it only in humorous ways. There is, for example, the banner that reads,

Let's be reasonable: do it my way. We can smile at it, but we know there is a truth in those mildly sardonic words. Many of us think that our way is the reasonable course; how could anything else be faintly reasonable?

The truth, of course, is that life is never reasonable and it seldom follows logical laws. A logical syllogism is not the model we follow in life. This does not mean that life is irrational or, according to the romantic theories of psychiatrist R. D. Laing, that we have hospitalized the sane people and let the crazies go free. To note that life is not reasonable is a way of understanding its true meaning. It defies systematic logic but only because it is complex and rich and the laws of intelligent thinking do not sum up all that goes into being human.

Not with a stranger

We may think that we are basically unreasonable only with people we do not know; this may explain the poisonous unreason of racial and religious prejudice. The fact is, however, that we are least reasonable with those who are closest to us.

Think of the husband and wife who say to each other, "Let's be reasonable about this." They may be many things with each other, but husbands and wives are seldom reasonable. If they are close their lives are anchored in a deep sea that runs with many emotional crosscurrents. Clear cold reason, the detached logic of an autopsy, may only be possible after a relationship is dead. It may, in fact, be the best sign that a relationship is not very deep, or that it is dying, and that it needs some of the stormy illogic of life breathed into it once more.

Friends may hammer out the expressions of their emotions on the anvil of rationalization, but they still possess only the outer shape of reason. Our explanations are generally not any more reasonable for having been so styled. Indeed, there are some friends who insist too much on a rational approach to friendship, on a courtroomlike adjudication of every slight, forgetfulness, or difficulty—accidental or otherwise. They can even bolster reason with justice. Too much talk like this means that the problem underlying the conflict is highly emotional, so emotional that one party at least prefers the torture of the reasonable approach to facing the experience of his or her inner emotions.

Our emotions are simply not susceptible to this kind of treatment. Neither friendship nor marriage can run very long or successfully on contractual logic. Reasonable arrangements written into the agreements between prospective marriage partners provide only an illusion of settling the conflicts that characteristically set the teeth of men and women on edge. In truth, such contracts—noting who does the dishes, walks the dog, buys the furniture, or decides on a vacation—treat only the occasions on which emotional conflicts may flare up. But if people are in conflict with each other, they find a way to express it no matter what fine print is contained in their signed and sealed agreements with each other. Our emotional selves defy logic and, in the long run, can easily destroy it and make its expensive-looking trappings appear shoddy. When people want to get at each other, they can always find ways to do so.

This is one of the problems connected with investing too much hope in reason as the best guide for handling strife in human affairs. It probably explains why the elaborate language of diplomacy was invented and is still used. This enables people to talk in public in a wonderful language that sounds like somebody is saying something when it is really designed to make sure that nobody's feelings are hurt. The language of diplomacy is an operational recognition of the emotional intricacies of dealing with the kinds of personal feelings—pride, anger, injured self-esteem—that seem to motivate nations. But does that language work for us as individuals?

The land of grudges

People who are in conflict sometimes don't speak any language to each other except that of silence. There may be a few grunts, a few formal requests exchanged, but the emotions within them are seldom expressed directly. They come out symbolically in many ways, not the least of which are the psychosomatic symptoms people experience when they are living with unresolved conflicts. Such people languish in a no man's land—dark, dreary and silent—which is the killing ground for friendship and marriage.

This land of grudges in which things are left unspoken is a place to which, unfortunately, we all retreat at times. We can even invoke logic to explain our being there. There are times when sulking is self-indulgent but we rationalize it by invoking things like "fair play" and other related virtues. Often enough people in this situation will not tell the people they believe to have wronged them just why they are irritated. They keep silent, leaving the other to guess what is wrong. Are there sadder sentences in the language than these: "I must have done something wrong but I don't know what it is," or "Well, I don't know what's bothering her/him now." It gets harder, in other words, for people to reach toward us with apologies or healing when we won't even tell them where it hurts. There is not much logic in that kind of intensely emotional withdrawal.

The language of emotions

Our real native language is that of the emotions—a tongue that is still Greek to many people. It is very helpful in ordinary living to understand that the real messages are not in the syntax but in the emotions that gave rise to them in the first place. When we realize that the language we speak is a vehicle more for feelings than for logic, we can begin to listen to ourselves and to others with greater understanding.

But we are not trying to deceive either ourselves or others. Just as we use phrases like To tell the truth, when we intend to exaggerate, so we are always sending and receiving indications of the way feelings contradict the sound of logic. We have to view ourselves totally, grasp the entire message, and translate it in terms of feeling as well as content in order to grasp where we, or others, stand. The clues are always there. If we are too committed to logic, we fail to spot them or we may completely disregard them. Our real messages are in our emotions, and no desire or even insistence on logic in human affairs can ever change that.

We are wiser . . .

. . . than our intellects, psychologist Carl Rogers once said. There is more to us than our conscious minds. Life is lived through the whole personality instead of any of the parts, no matter how important these may be. When we understand this we are far more comfortable with ourselves and with other persons. We begin to catch the pattern in our self-presentation that points to the conflicting emotion of some other struggle beneath our spoken words. We begin to listen to the kind of stories we tell or to the examples we give with a new understanding that these are efforts to reveal to ourselves and others what we are really feeling. We are trying to make ourselves present as truthfully as possible, but the message is complex and subtle and it may take us some time to feel it and to hear it fully. Yet there is plenty of time to do this; the problem is not available time. It centers rather on our willingness to surrender the hard and fast laws of logic in order to understand a deeper logic by which human beings express themselves to each other.

Understanding this helps us avoid defeat and frustration. When we know what is going on at the deeper levels of our personality, we always do much better. We can then grasp the real issues. We can read between the lines of life and find its meaning bold and clear. There is common sense in this approach. But, of course, common sense is more than logic, too.

Why they invented love

It is clear that the only response that can enable us to live in a world where illogic seems to have such power is that of love, the substance that is not just sentimental or merely mindlessly romantic. It matches the complexities of our human personalities. Love enables us to bring the best of ourselves together in response to what can seem the constantly bewildering realities of unreasonable existence. It is not a bad thing to remember as we begin more surely to make our way through a new year.

Perhaps it has never been said better than by Robert Bolt in *A Man for All Seasons:*

> If we lived in a state where virtue was profitable, common sense would make us good, and greed would make us saintly. And we'd live like animals or angels in a happy land that *needs* no heroes. But since, in fact, we see that avarice, anger, envy, bribery, sloth, lust and stupidity commonly profit far beyond humility, chastity, fortitude, justice and thought, and have to choose, to be human at all . . . why then perhaps stand fast a little . . . even at the risk of being heroes. . . . It isn't a matter of reason; finally, it's a matter of love.

Things that are okay

When we are even a little more tolerant of our lot as human beings, we find that many of the things that we once thought were terrible are really okay. We know, for example, that it is all right to be angry, that there is no intrinsic evil connected with having strong emotions. Most people have also learned by now that it is not surprising to have a wild fantasy life. Having one doesn't mean that the fantasies are going to be acted out or that those who have fantasies need treatment. People have come to understand many of these things, but there are many other aspects of their experiences that are perfectly permissible as well. Among them:

It is okay not to feel guilty because you are not a commando in the sexual revolution. Many persons feel intimidated because they are neither thinking of nor doing the things some magazines, talk shows, and other media tell us "modern" people talk about and do. They feel that they are out of step because they are not really interested in orgies, wife swapping, or even changing their own sexual lives to conform to what experts tell them are richer and better ways of expressing and enjoying themselves. But it is all right not to be caught up in the tide of currently favored sexual attitudes or practices. It really is okay to feel at peace with the adjustment that one has made through experience and some reciprocal tenderness in life. It is all right, really; it is unnecessary to change oneself to conform to the current folklore on the subject.

It is even okay to be forgiving rather than incessantly condemning of the institutions in our society that catch most of the lightning, frequently quite deservedly, for their failure to be more responsive to human needs. These include not only government and education but also the churches whose imperfection was a well-kept secret for years. Many people are very tired of the bitterness—perhaps the greatest backlash of our times—that has been directed against church institutions in recent years. It is all right to forgive churches for not being as faultless as we once believed. It is acceptable to view them more realistically and to want them to do better, to believe in them because of the possibilities of service which are still theirs. It is okay, in other words, to feel that going to church and belonging to a community of believers is still a good thing, even when they fall as far short of the ideal as we do.

It is also okay to believe in marriage and the family, institutions that have been under constant attack and under the dark cloud of prediction generated by future shock prophets for several years now. To hear the seers talk, short-term companionate marriages will be the only style quite shortly. Living with the same person for a lifetime seems an impossible and boring prospect to these experts, and yet marriage and the family have survived a great deal of history and they are likely to survive the future. For all their imperfections, they are still institutions in which human beings thrive, and they offer the stability of custom and relationship that most people long for.

It is all right to stand for something even when one's own children or students test you by rejecting or seeming to reject so many of your values. Some older people quickly run for cover when this happens; this does not convince the young, and it is personally unsatisfying. It is even all right to discipline one's children or students in a consistent and commonsense way. People who hold back from this out of fear that they are going to traumatize their children by any cross words simply do not understand life or the toughness of kids. They do more damage by inaction than by some timely and healthy correction. One should not underestimate the resiliency of the young; they can absorb just punishments and never show any scars at all.

It is okay to believe in fidelity, and it is not bad to believe in working out whatever difficulties friendship and love bring in order to preserve this value. In the age of the no-fault divorce and the presumably therapeutic affair, some people have tried to make a virtue out of avoiding commitments to each other. We have nothing new in this; people have done it all through history and it has never improved the general situation. Couples do develop, however, by working at understanding fidelity and by working together through difficulties that are now fashionable merely to dodge or run away from. It is still okay to believe that being true to each other, with whatever suffering such growth entails, is one of the best things that can happen to people.

It is still okay to believe in love and its possibilities even when people like to tell us that love is more illusion than reality. But despite all this, people believe in and give themselves generously to love; they find it persistently a part of their lives, the richest source of their meaning, and a key to understanding the universe. There is really nothing wrong with this; and to distrust such a conviction is to run the risk of destroying one's happiness.

It is okay, in general, to be old-fashioned, out of step, and sometimes out of style. These are things that happen to people who bet on values that are deeper than the newest color lipstick, the latest width of tie, or dressing like a safari guide when one is really a businessman in a big city. In the final analysis, they constitute the surface of life, and people who are deeply involved in life do not have much time for worrying about how they look. But it is all right to be that forgetful because it may provide firsthand evidence that an individual is living a purposeful life, that one's relationships are more than casual, and that one has indeed discovered the treasure for which others have not yet found the map.

Something to remember

Although we live in a world where progress is highly valued, there are not many advances that really improve things. There have been wonderful discoveries, of course, but each one of them brings a new kind of liability. Wonder drugs gave rise to tougher germs; efficient insecticides killed far more than the bugs they were designed to eliminate. The century that witnessed the invention of the auto, the plane, and the rocket finds that one of its major problems is mass transportation. There is hardly anything new—no matter how it is advertised—that doesn't have a new and improved flaw connected with it. Air conditioners are noisy, the newest of cars is recalled for defects, and even the newest houses and buildings have unsuspected creaks, groans, and failings that are only discovered after people move into them. Improvements, in other words, bring modernized imperfections as much as they bring progress. That is why we can be suspicious when a product is advertised as "new and improved."

With things or people we will always find something wrong. But this truth, especially concerning people, is part of what is right about them. They would be dreadfully wrong if they had no problems at all or if they offered no problems to us. There is nothing wrong with being sinful but there is everything wretched in not being able to forgive ourselves and each other for it.

Let's not talk about it

Communicating and confessing are supposed to be good for human beings. If we can only get it out, other people tell us, we will feel much better. That's popular psychological gospel, and it is second nature that it even seems like common sense.

But we all know that there are times when we are not so sure about this advice, when, for whatever reason, we are not only unwilling but unable to talk about something that causes us pain. It seems that our souls might splinter if we squeeze them for every ounce of the truth; we would rather hold still than make any move or sound that might make our anguish worse. We don't want to talk about it, we say, and sometimes this is not such a bad idea. There are lessons to be learned about ourselves and others here.

The urgers

First, a few words about urgers, a group we can all fall into very easily. Urgers are a confident band of advisers, absolutely positive that others should unburden themselves to them. Such people, always sure that they are good-hearted, never question the principle that getting the truth out of others is a good thing. The most obvious question to ask centers on their certainty that they know what is best for others. This requires enormous presumption on anybody's part, especially when it concerns tender spots in our psyches. How can any of us be sure when and where to probe into another person's life? Persons do this—like a drunk trying a high wire walk—only when they simply don't know enough to sense the danger. And yet some people do it all the time and never wonder whether they have made things worse in the process.

It is very easy to become an urger, however, and you can usually recognize these people by some of the familiar phrases they use as they step gingerly away from the disasters they cause. "I was only trying to be helpful," they will say, a vague presentiment of failure coloring the tone of their voices. Ah, the sins committed under that banner are yet to be numbered. Or how about, "I was only doing this for *your* good," as they move rapidly away from the ruin they have caused.

All we have to do is look into our own lives to see how we feel when somebody else pushes too hard at something that hurts deep within us. That memory may be enough to make us hesitate about doing the same kind of thing to somebody else.

Second cousins

Closely akin to urgers are the persons who seem to worry about us too much. They may not say much but they make their concern clear. They have little evidence but they manage to think the worst of us.

It is a demeaning experience to be misunderstood or misjudged in this way. We discover that somebody confidently expects that we will fail or fall even though they may only admit this in the context of saying that they are praying for us. It is strange that the promise of a prayer can sometimes be the seal of an unforgiving judgment on our behavior and motivations.

There is no way in which we can justify ourselves to these people, because they are convinced that they possess the truth and no testimony of ours can dissuade them. The best we can hope for is that they will do us the courtesy of leaving us alone. Sometimes we have to settle for that; it certainly beats getting treated like a sinner. In addition to avoiding people who do this to us, we can now, in golden-rule fashion, never do this to others.

And as for us

What do we do when we do not want to talk about something? It is not something we can easily hide; we human beings simply do not work that way. We typically let our conflict out indirectly, thinking we can successfully look away from it and that others won't notice. One of the things we may do is become depressed. This always shows, of course, and is by pain itself defined; when we feel bad and can't talk about it, we solve our problem by feeling worse. It is a curious system, but we humans cannot seem to break away from using it. We are forever exchanging pains, trading off fear for anxiety, or the blues for the hard truth.

Knowing this about ourselves enables us to understand that we can never really get very far away from something that is rankling in our innards. We may process it differently or adjust to it in an altered manner, but we never blot it out. It remains there, a living part of us, but when we can admit it to our consciousness, we can stop working so hard at hiding it. This removes a lot of tension from the situation and gives us a little more breathing space. And it is in this space that we often find both the peace and the courage to face what is in conflict within us.

Waiting for ourselves

Life is filled with the lessons of waiting, but the hardest may be when we have to wait for ourselves. Sometimes our own urge to get problems settled makes us push too hard at trying to extract the truth from ourselves. We want to be over it, out of the valley of shadows and back into life again. But that cannot be a hurried journey and it certainly is as miserable as a forced march.

There are many occasions when we must wait until we are ready inside before we can speak the words of our problem even to ourselves. It is okay for others to have headaches and bad days, but we don't want to grant ourselves permission for these common human ailments.

There has been a great deal of interest lately in the idea of learning how to be your own best friend. A large element of this is in giving ourselves time for the pains that we are not yet strong enough to talk about or wise enough to heal. There are many experiences we have to suffer until we can see them in a clear enough light to identify them for ourselves. We are more weak and fragile than we want to admit. Our strength builds when we don't get angry with ourselves because we are so human. Getting past this, however, we can draw closer to whatever is bothering us, because we feel less threatened and less ashamed of it.

Being able to listen in the quiet moments of waiting we grant to ourselves allows us to hear ourselves without having to be condemned or punished in the process. There is indeed a time for weeping, and it cannot be hurried.

This is not to say that things should remain bottled up inside us forever; they only grow more sour or explode when we deny them the light and air of expression. But things cannot be torn from us out of due time. Just as with the birth of a child or a great idea, there is no shortcut to the processes of development and consolidation by which the layers of our disrupted emotions come together so that we may speak them aloud. When we can acknowledge without distortion the source of our conflict, we are more alive; there is literally more of us present after this painful acknowledgment of the truth about ourselves. This is because the wound is part of us but, until the right moment, we will be more tempted to deny than to acknowledge this or we will distort it to calm ourselves. But calming ourselves is not the same as healing ourselves.

Healing comes when we are able, with the perspectives that waiting gives us, to appraise ourselves more openly. This is an aspect of the mystery of revelation, an example of the way we make ourselves whole.

Making room for each other

People who want to understand life know something about waiting both for themselves and for others. It does not look like much from the outside, in a country eager for action, but just waiting for others in an active way is a powerful and life-giving experience. If people who try to get us to talk when we would prefer to remain quiet resemble dentists with bad judgment about which teeth to pull, the others—those who wait with and for us in our times of anguish—are living sources of grace. It only looks like they are not doing much; this, however, is a real characteristic of some of our most vital passages together. A parent sitting up with a sick child may not seem very active; neither do friends who are close enough to be quiet together. Yet life leaps like light across these scenes.

Making room for each other means creating enough space around us so that people can feel our presence and yet, at the same time, feel free in it. It is an extraordinary thing to feel bad and not be able to talk about it, but still to be with somebody who gives us the room to be that way. Such a person senses something about the inner process that has to occur for us to face the pains and mistakes of our days.

Those who press us unyieldingly make us defensive; we look to them more for excuses than for the truth. They often heighten our discomfort while insisting that they only want to lessen it. They take away more than they give with all their corrupt and insensitive good intentions.

Far different is the situation in which we can be still with our sorrow until we are strong enough to speak the words that free us from it. We are able to do this because there is somebody *there* ready to listen yet tender enough to let us find our own words at our own pace. There are few things more anguishing than a conflict that is smoldering and still too hot to approach. We can feel the intensity of its heat, and yet we seem powerless to do much but let it happen.

This is the kind of pain that makes us feel our loneliness in a new and intense way, as though we were all by ourselves, strangers almost to the universe. At these times those who give us their presence—neither shaming nor probing us—are like the blessing of a cooling rain. They feed us in the quiet and strengthen us by standing nearby in a space large enough for both of us. Blessed are they who understand and wait with us, for they give us back our souls.

CHAPTER 8

A time to seek and a time to lose
A time to keep and a time to cast
away . . .

Questions! Questions!

Everybody wants some answers, and straight talk at that. That is what they say during an election year, anyway, and that is probably why hindsight has come close to canonizing Harry Truman for supposedly offering us both during his years in office. Perhaps that is so. But is our image of him enhanced somewhat by a projection of our own needs for something definite, for our pilgrim's longing, after so much land has given way under our feet, for solid ground that will bear our weight at last? And life remains filled with questions—some good, some bad, and some just rhetorical. They range from the one for $64,000 to the death-bed inquiry of Gertrude Stein: "But what is the question?" What are we to make of it all?

Second nature

The fact that we do not have as many answers as we have questions should not dismay us. Curiosity, because of the fable about the cat, has an undeservedly bad reputation. It is, in fact, one of our most essential—indeed, charming—characteristics. There would be no survival, perhaps there would never have been an emergence from the cave by our prehistoric ancestors, if nobody asked about what was out there anyway. History would have frozen as still as a subzero winter morning without the spirit of inquiry that remains one of our most vital attributes.

Our need to question explains a variety of things about us, including distractions at prayer, because we are always searching about ourselves, if we are healthy, with a wonder that takes us on exhilarating and fulfilling journeys. The human person might be defined as the only questioner in the universe. Our passion for inquiry not only sells newspapers but gives us a feeling for the still uncharted shape of the future that billows in the darkness around us.

Life, we aver, would be more comfortable without so many questions at times. Yes, but it might become constricted and dull, the dry and brittle existence that is the inheritance of the fearful. Curiosity is not vanity but a human quality that ignites and gives support to our capacity for growth. That is why it is related to creativity. The authentically creative person does not copy but rather follows his or her questions wherever they may lead. Their art is the shape of their answer, whether it comes out as an invention, a novel, or a marble statue. These are the gifts that questioning spirits share with the rest of us, the tentative answers that are the directional markers of culture. None of this could happen without a spirit of questioning at the root of it all.

And questions are related to our religious experience as well. Religious faith has been described on a continuum of development. Faith that is not fully grown, faith that is just the beginning of faith, tries to supply us with answers, securely attacking the special fabric of interpretation, like swaddling clothes, around the universe itself. A more developed religious faith, however, does not concern itself quite so much with answers. This form of faith, researchers tell us, does not provide answers but asks more questions. It builds on our spirit of inquiry, inviting us to take further steps on our journey into ourselves and into our world. Questioning in the context of religious faith is not the same as raising destructive doubts about religious truths. It is the only way in which we can travel to the core of what we believe, the only way we can journey to the fullness of ourselves.

Questions may be disordering; they always are parts of our

adjustment, cracking it like a steel ball hitting concrete. Questions dislodge us from positions into which we have settled, forcing us to move on toward higher ground. Questioning, associated with religious belief, bids us to make ourselves whole at a higher level and in a richer way. Dying and rising are sown into our inquiries, giving us a daily experience of the central mystery of faith. We die to ourselves as we look more deeply into the directions in which we have not yet gone; in that direction, however, lies a richer life, the joy beyond mere fulfillment of becoming more of who we really are.

Faith and trust

Questions are not, then, the enemy but the condition for faith. Faith has never been merely that which provides us with a well-stocked bunker in which we can find ourselves secure against life. It generates rather the energy of spirit to face life without every last snippet of comforting answer or explanation; faith allows us to live with questions, with things unresolved. Such belief is a dynamic characteristic of healthy existence with ourselves, with God and with each other.

A special form of faith is seen in trust, that invisible ribbon that ties us, like an astronaut's lifeline, to each other and through which we nourish each other with our daily supply of human strength.

Truth is unquestioning, they say, but is it? What strength can trust have if we do not recognize or never taste the bitter rind of human weakness? Trust is the thing that goes with our imperfect condition, the substance that makes us strong even though the way is dark and unsure, the swaying bridge across the abyss of every day. Trust is not trust if it is not filled with unanswered questions.

Can parents be without questions as they allow their children to go out on their own, even in something as simple as letting them have the keys to the car for the first time? Can lovers not worry or wonder about the dangers that hang like clouds over them while they are apart? How strong can trust be if it is fully armed against questions? Trust works because it makes us open-ended to persons as they try to forge their own answers to the large questions of life. Trust makes us available, in a very real but unseen way, as a source of support for all those we love.

Questions without answers

Inquiry is part of our noblest heritage, but we have to come to terms with the fact that we cannot answer, nor can anyone else, some of our best questions. They are not rhetorical questions, however, because they are not asked for effect or to prove a point. They are questions tinged with mystery, inquiries that involve us not in vain or superficial wondering, but in the meaning of our own lives. These are questions we ask all the time, when we are brave enough, questions that wait to be asked and that rumble in our unconscious if we do not put them into words. These are the questions for every day. But we sometimes only have the strength—or are forced—to ask them on certain heightened occasions when we can look away from them no longer.

Such a question, for example, is occasioned for parents when their first child leaves home. Parents ask, although seldom out loud, something like this: *Have I loved him enough? Have I loved her enough?* Inquiries almost too big for the heart, the questions that define us and yet whose answers lie beyond our grasp in that shaded area of unaudited trust in which we finally have to let go of things and persons and let them be on their own. But who can fail to know the searchings of the heart beneath such a question, or the potential for guilt if a person cannot live without a more reassuring answer? Not one of us—as a parent, a teacher, or a friend—is immune from the doubts about the full truth of our love. There is a question at the very heart of the mystery of separation, that strange inescapable experience that lives at the edge of love. When we must separate or are separated—and how many times this happens in large or small ways —these questions come close to the surface of our awareness. We have done our best, we say, and yet we can also see the things we have left undone, the small graces withheld for no particular reason, the chances we ignored or avoided, the whole raw material of regret that we cannot allow to smother us if we are to move forward. And yet there the questions are, waiting for answers and unanswerable all at the same time, a measure for us of whether we are growing into something more or into something less in life.

A similar question is this: *Is this the right thing to do?* Behind this query is the complex moral inventory we take when we are in conflict or when we have mixed motives. It becomes a heavy burden if we cannot live without some loose edges on existence or if we must be absolutely certain that we have done the correct thing in every set of circumstances. We can never, of course, be totally without question as far as our decisions go. One wonders if there would be any fiber in a moral decision if there were no margin for error, no chance that we could be wrong, that necessary chance we take again and again when, by the lights we have, we sign our names to our lives through the choices we make.

Yet another question asks: *Why did this happen?* We can ask it at every turn in our journey. Who can save us from this question in a world where the void echoes with inquiry but gives back few direct answers? Indeed, are not our prayers, insofar as they reflect our deepest and most honest searching of ourselves, really questions of this sort? Are we not always mystified to some extent even when our faith tells us that there is a meaning beyond the immediate fact of illness, tragedy, or injustice? Why do the innocent suffer and why do the wicked prosper? And why has this happened to me? These are questions to which we make some answer by the very fact that we are willing to ask them. They help us to discern our self-pity and then uncover unsuspected sources of courage; they give us back perspective and something of our souls. These are the questions that tell us we have tasted life, that we have not missed it, that we have cared enough for others and for life to be concerned or hurt or bewildered.

It is questioning that leads to a deeper faith and an acceptance and affirmation of life that is based not on a sugar-coated vision of it, but on the unretouched facts of existence. These are the questions for a pilgrim people. They can still walk through the valley of the shadow of death unafraid, because they live by a faith that acquaints them with rather than protects them from the dangers all around them.

What was it I wanted to buy?

There is a powerful scene in Eugene O'Neill's *Long Day's Journey Into Night* (New Haven: Yale University Press, 1956) in which the old actor, James Tyrone, caught up in a dialogue with his tubercular son, recalls his life and, for a moment at least, confronts the puzzle of his miserliness. Tightening a light bulb that, through the habit of a lifetime, he had previously loosened in order to save money, he speaks half to his son and half to himself. His other son is an alcoholic and his wife a drug addict. "What the hell was it I wanted to buy, I wonder, that was worth . . ." he asks himself but he cannot seem to find an answer. "Well, no matter. It's a late day for regrets." He talks on about his earlier career, only to return to this same theme, shaking his head as though he could not find something that should be close at hand. "No, I don't know what the hell it was I wanted to buy."

The world has suddenly grown aware of the mid-life crisis, that slight mound that is less than a mountain from which people can look back at life in mid-journey. Perhaps we all have reasons for some regrets about the way our lives have gone. The worst variety are like those of James Tyrone. He has waited and saved, denied and wasted himself and others; now he is not even sure why. The old actor feels that it is too late even for regrets, that he cannot undo the investments whose purpose now elude him. And so he must live with the wreckage of a world that he keeps at a distance through drink and reruns of his daydreams.

The first signs of autumn are something like middle age, offering us a place and a time to look both backward and forward at our lives. Regrets never solve anything, of course; even modest resolves save many lives from the kind of fatalistic bitterness that can bring us, not knowing what we saved our energies for, to say along with the old actor, "No, I don't know what the hell it was I wanted to buy. . . ."

What do we want to buy?

In a consumer society that is nonetheless filled with frustrations and shortages, the question might better be phrased, What *can* we buy? The deeper inquiry for the thoughtful asks, What is of value in my life? Our society has great concern about inflation and how to find those investments that will make money grow faster than the price of everything else. Some popular contemporary values are as fragile and distended as balloons; and we can only survive, in an inflated environment, if the investments of our person are in values that are rich in the right things and, therefore, lasting.

To discover where our treasure is, we must, as the Scriptures tell us, find out where our hearts are. In other words, what makes a difference to us in life? What moves us to action or to make sacrifices? What, indeed, are the truths we live by? What do we believe in? Is it progress, the notion that things keep getting better whether we do anything about them or not? Or is it music, as a now almost forgotten popular song once suggested? Maybe it is success, or have we seen too many unhappy faces in an affluent land?

What are we saving ourselves for?

It is true that persons who have known want in their early years —such as persons who may have lived through the Great Depression—find that they cannot just let themselves go as freely as they would like, either in finance or in friendship. The possibility of losing everything is too real, because they can remember, even faintly, times when they barely had enough to get by. It would be foolish not to recognize these psychological roots, which may run very deep and also explain at least some of their problems. One would be foolish indeed to think that a sudden and radical transformation of a style that was learned in painful circumstances can take place overnight.

We must begin realistically with some recognition and acceptance of the way we have invested ourselves in life. If we have been too saving—too oriented toward security—then we may be able to free ourselves a little bit so that we can enjoy life more and make it possible for others to enjoy it more as well. Compromise may be the psychological order of the day for persons who discover that our hearts have been hardened to such an extent that they can barely be broken into at the present time. The answer, as it has always been, is that hard hearts open only from within. It is also true that even a small amount of openness—a little greater willingness to risk ourselves—causes a very large increase in our own happiness.

It is very hard to believe in anything or in anyone if our imagination is dominated by an overblown need for security. If we cannot give ourselves or our possessions away unless we are absolutely certain of the outcome of everything we do, we deny ourselves the fundamental experiences that enable us to know who we are. There is a big difference in the kinds of treasures that gladden men's hearts. Some people desire concrete things that can be counted and stored away; these are usually cold and are kept in the dark under lock and key. Others recognize that the only things that matter are not concrete, cannot be counted, and cannot really be seen much less stored away safely. These abiding values center on whether we put other people and their growth and development first; whether, in other words, we understand that loving God and loving our neighbor are bound up together. There is no way to do either unless we are willing to spend freely rather than just make tax-exempt deductions on the gift of ourselves in life.

A believer—in God, in life, and in love—never ends up standing in the wreckage of life asking, "What the hell was it I wanted to buy, I wonder, what was worth. . . . Well, no matter, it's a late day for regrets. . . ."

Getting what you want

The question is: How many people do? Have we ever lived at a time in which persons spoke so much about fulfillment, sought it more eagerly, and seemed to miss it more spectacularly? We may yet go down in history as the generation that worked hardest at finding itself only to discover, with more than a few regrets, that it looked in all the wrong places.

Fulfillment is the word of the age, and yet many have a corrupt notion of its meaning. It has been operationally translated as putting oneself first, no matter what commitments are thereby endangered and no matter who is hurt. Fulfillment, however, can never flow from a totally selfish basis. Personal fulfillment depends on our learning to respect the truth not only about ourselves but about all those who are close to us. A sense of fulfillment is an illusion in the life of a person who has not learned how to love.

But that is precisely the difficulty. It is gratifyingly smug to sing, "I did it my way," but the person who wants to stop kidding himself understands that a happy life depends on learning always to do things *our way*. We grow in and through relationships with others; we cannot take all the oxygen in our living space just for ourselves. We may sing, "I gotta be me," but we will never make the journey to our true selves all alone.

Placing our needs and wants in first place no matter what it means in terms of sacrifices or psychic injury to others is to live an infantile dream. The sad part about the careless use of fulfillment as an excuse, for example, to break up families—and lots of hearts in the process—is that the romantic notion that doing a heroic thing on our own can easily turn into a ravaging experience of aloneness. It means isolation and hurt for the person who strikes out alone and for those, especially children, left behind.

This is not to deny the importance of some of the overdue hard choices of life. These can include the maturing person who shifts to a more suitable career or location or even goal. It is hard, however, to imagine that breaking the hearts of a lot of other people along the way can ever justify our own development. The fact is that such psychological carnage is presently being rationalized on a wide scale in our society. We don't find ourselves by abandoning others; we still discover who we are more by letting go of rather than holding on to ourselves.

Does everybody get what they want?

It is a fair question to ask in a generation that counts longing as an everyday experience. Long ago Oscar Wilde had a character say: "In this world there are only two tragedies. One is not getting what one wants, and the other is getting it." Indeed, it is a time to reflect on what we are looking for in life and on the means we choose to secure it.

"More!" is what the old union leader is supposed to have replied when asked what the workers would want. And that, in the same undifferentiated sense, is what many Americans have sought as well. Maintaining the balance between more and less may sum up the art of living. We disrespect ourselves as persons when we ignore the conscious choices that must go into keeping that balance.

There are some things we desperately need more of; these include sensitivity and understanding as well as tenderness and compassion. These are the very things which ask us to make less of ourselves so that there is more room close to us for others. And we could use less of noisy self-assertion, narcissistic personal absorption, and the twin devils of envy and greed. These are the blind forces that seek more for us at the price of making less of us.

The things we actually need in order to become more considerate and loving persons only seem to ask us to be less than we are. In truth the pursuit of these qualities strips us of the selfishness that remains our greatest obstacle to fulfillment and happiness. We can never get enough of what we seek only for ourselves. But we still find everything we need when we understand that we never do anything really loving or lasting by insisting on doing it "my way."

Something more to us

We are a mixture of longings, of idealizations and grand plans, of decisions about what we will do or what we will be like after we have achieved this or that objective. And we achieve the objective and we are, strangely but consistently, not as content as we had supposed. Often enough we are restless, already spying yet greener pastures on the other side of the fence that is just beyond us.

There may be no experience more common than the delight of anticipation and the slight discount at which reality finally sells. There is no grander moment, for example, than the start of a happy journey and no greater frustration than not being able to hold on to that special experience of exhilaration. "I come upon no wine," Edna St. Vincent Millay once wrote, "so wonderful as thirst." There is a hint of a destiny beyond ourselves in all our moments of yearning. We catch a fleeting glimpse of eternity in all our broken moments of time; we sense the depths of our spiritual possibilities in the longing that edges the best of our human experiences. It is one of the languages God uses to speak softly to us.

We always have something to learn about ourselves and who we might yet be. There is no season like summer for these feelings—the time of ripeness and fulfillment, the season we look forward to only to feel it slipping away from us as we try to grasp it. We understand ourselves better when we can enter into the poignancy of our lives, learning from rather than regretting the hints we constantly receive that we are made finally to transcend all our broken moments in eternal life.

The surface of things

It is at once the pain and the preoccupation of our culture. We are, to some extent at least, absorbed with surfaces, with effects and appearances, with the winking glint of polished brass as much as the glitter of diamonds, with the cleverness of photographiclike art that seems to make flat walls give way to winding paths and old-fashioned streets, with the outside of bodies even in a land that speaks about its missing fullness of personhood. Somehow we have become transfixed with appearances, with the way things look far more than the way things actually are, with the backdrop for our lives more than the substance of our living. Is this at least a partial source of our existential discontent? Or is it rather a symptom of a deeper loss that we have not yet learned to identify, much less to mourn?

Surfaces are a fine art, for example, in our entertainments, in our movies filled with the special effects of disasters as well as the recreation of other eras. Everything is right, the set designers proudly tell us, as they did, for example, about the Boston mansion of the once highly anticipated television series "Beacon Hill." Even the grocery lists and bills hanging in the kitchen were inscribed with correct purchases and charges for the goods and services of post–World War One America. Such passion for detail was not, however, evident in the development of the characters of the Irish family that supposedly lived in those surroundings. Its members were shallow caricatures, their dramatic failure merely highlighted by the perfect surfaces of their sets. And, of course, the series faltered and died of terminal insubstantiality.

And so it is with a number of popular films. Perhaps *Barry Lyndon* is the chief example of the lush re-creation of the surfaces—of the feel, if you will—of another era, of paintings and etchings come alive, of the flickering look of candlelit dinners in great houses, of the jumble of cities two hundred years ago—an astonishing accomplishment and one that cried out for a story about persons of greater depth than those who stand before those impressive backgrounds. There was even a special sting in *The Sting*, a movie that so lovingly re-created Chicago in 1936 as the textured setting for a pleasant but hardly profound tale of con men. I have, in fact, heard Chicagoans arguing about the exact locales used for many of the scenes; the lingering sting is that most of it was filmed in San Pedro, California.

More serious, of course, is the politics of appearance that has come to dominate our election years. Candidates have to have a certain "look," and it cannot be too old or too young. Half the candidates are covering up gray hair while the other half are adding a distinguished touch or edge of it here or there. And so the speeches are frequently tailored for effect, for manipulation on the surface rather than for engagement at a deeper level.

The politics of appearance are, of course, hardly limited to politicians in a land in which so many people try to let their costumes speak for them when they cannot speak for themselves. Making everything look right kills the possibility of a deeper honesty, even with ourselves. Just get it right on the outside and it is easier to deny the implications of what we really feel or do on the inside. Talk about behavior rather than human consciousness; measure it rather than reflect on it. That is a prescription for living on the surface of things, a hint of an explanation for the metaphysical pain of so many people who hunger and thirst for a special kind of justice, the right to experience their own humanity in depth.

One of the worst betrayals of pornography is its unyielding emphasis on surfaces, on the flesh devoid of spirit, on the contours and planes of the erotic, on the curves and lines and the panes and facings of the body. Here is sacrilege; the beauty of the human body is marred because the inner qualities of the person are purposely ignored in these slick illusions of seduction. Pornography is more than boring because in the name of showing us everything about humans, it conceals what is most distinguishing.

And that, of course, is why so much increased emphasis on sexual pleasure—pleasure is, after all, a word of the surface—has seemed to yield so little lasting happiness—happiness is, after all, a word of depth. We are trying to get from the surface what the surface cannot possibly yield; it is like trying to get nourishment or find human response from a plastic chair. This preoccupation with surfaces, according to psychoanalyst Otto Kernberg, is a major impediment to a person's capacity to fall in love. Relationships are neither initiated nor sustained by surface tension. And that is why the false promises of appearances, sex out of context, and shallow fulfillment are so crushing to persons who want, perhaps more than anything else, an experience of deep and lasting love.

But how do you get into life more deeply, that is the question, and how do you manage to stay there successfully? We are surrounded by movements that offer the promise of a deeper experience of the self; they range from aspects of human potential strivings to the self-contained assertiveness of *est*. There are programs with more spiritual-sounding titles as well; they propose exercises in meditation or relaxation, prayer and contemplation. One can understand why people flock to these movements, conscientiously attempting to break through to a richer level of experience.

And yet we need travel no great distance to find a place of entry into deeper life. These experiences are not just around the corner or over the horizon; they are not *out there* waiting for us to find them, by will or by chance, and be transformed by them. They are at hand all the time, and our passage to a deeper sense of ourselves is made in and through the effort we must make to respond in these situations. We come alive in these circumstances, because they cut through our fragile surface bindings to test something deeper in us. These are not experiences we can fake our way through by some rearrangement of our surface qualities. Our looks don't make much difference when the issue centers on our hearts.

Such experiences include events that, in the name of a more placid existence or some species of Far Eastern calm, many people attempt to overcome or exclude from their lives. Take anxiety, for example, that bubbling reading of our emotional temperature, that cowardly thief of the dark and quiet hours who robs us of sleep and concentration, tugging at our consciousness with reminders of the unfinished business of our existence. Anxiety seems an enemy to a tranquilized society, and yet if we pause for a moment to search out its roots we may discover that it is more of a signal flag than a banner of mourning. It tells us something about ourselves, a squeak in the hinges of the psyche to draw our attention to something we need to inspect more carefully.

But who wants to worry, or feel guilty or uneasy? Are these not old-fashioned behaviors, mustily Victorian at best? Anxiety is a sound from inside ourselves and it means that we are alive and engaged in human things. It is true that many of our worries are not very consequential; they disappear, or at least diminish, when we inspect them. And they are sometimes of great significance because they are evidence of the human cost of being close to others or of trying our strengths creatively in life.

There are always things unfinished and other things that need to be begun.

This, indeed, is the texture of everyday existence in which moments of serenity are granted infrequently and for severely limited periods. Beware the life of no anxiety, of no stirring of concern or care; we are ready for burial when we have drained our existence of passion; we are fit then only for formaldehyde. There is a healthy uneasiness connected with any purposeful activity; we are at our best when we are slightly off balance. Indeed, the deepest of our experiences are only possible when we are dislodged from a too comfortable encampment.

We only need to believe—that is, to test our faith and its fiber —when we live between the known and the unknown, between reality and possibility, in that small lively space between now and the future. When, for example, does believing in others make a difference both to us and to them? We don't tax our faith in fair weather but we have to let out the lines every day during the yawing of human relationships in, for example, our moments of misunderstanding or disappointment with others, in the moments when we are injured and need to forgive, or when we seek pardon and need forgiveness. The prize of the inside of life is yielded to those who are ready to believe in these circumstances; they live deeply through the effort to enter into rather than avoid such experiences.

So parents are tried a thousand ways in maintaining rather than abandoning faith in their children, who grow different and more mysterious every day. Lovers keep in relationship through the seasons of changes and discoveries, great and small, that fill their lives. Anybody who cares truly about anybody or anything knows the edge of dread that all can go wrong or can be lost or damaged seriously at any moment. That is the fire on the horizon of any engaged existence, the evidence of a life whose roots reach far beneath the surface.

The moments of truth abound in the average life. They are not spectacular; the earth doesn't move and the sun doesn't spin in the sky. They are not moments of great enlightenment because most of them are shrouded in semi-darkness; they are not interludes of undisturbed peace, because tumult is part of everything human enough to move our depths. They are as simple as everything that goes into raising a child or keeping a friend, as common as growing up or growing old, as compelling as doing hard work or facing hard truths. We are surrounded with the opportunities for depth all the time and we need not postpone our commitment to them. The trembling that accompanies anything important makes a demand on our faith—and that is the solid core of the faith that makes us whole.

Kinky fantasies

The latest example of twentieth-century people turning themselves inside out in the name of achieving modernity, acceptance, or a species of self-esteem lies in the effort to produce kinky sexual fantasies. This is presumably a prelude to sexual activity, and it has somehow gotten around in the culture that the kinkier the fantasies, the more sophisticated the persons involved.

People think they must produce sexual fantasies to order, and the more bizarre the better. That is the "in" thing, and people who do not spontaneously experience these fantasies are made to feel out of it. It sounds, to the modern ear, old-fashioned to doubt even mildly or to question this contemporary notion at all. But, for the moment, let's be old-fashioned and, with human common sense, say that such notions are crazy and they result only in the intimidation of the normal and healthy men and women in the population.

It may even be time to resurrect an old-fashioned word, *lust,* and wonder whether we have not so idealized its experience at this time that we have lost sight of its raw meaning. Lust has become the guiltless preoccupation of a culture that has a great deal of difficulty in putting itself in order. Lust may not be the worst of sins but it is not exactly the peak moment of human experience either.

True peak moments come in work that is purposeful, in relationships that are loving, and in life that is lived from the inside. Lust and the kinky fantasies that are meant to generate it emphasize the surface of things and they leave people tied up inside of themselves all hot and bothered, as they used to say, but curiously remote and cold within, strangely out of focus, and hard to reach in a human fashion. This is because the development of kinky fantasies is an aspect of narcissism that has been licensed in a culture that has lost its moorings.

The sad part is that people who think they can lead their lives solely in search of erotic satisfactions for themselves end up lonely, not because they do not want love but because they have never learned where to look for it. They peer too much within themselves, and it makes it impossible for them to see other persons clearly. That may be why they deform others in the fantasies of their sexual confusion. They thereby destroy the tenderness of loving sexual communication and make themselves more remote from a deeply satisfying and happy experience of life.

Warning: do-gooders sighted lately

The Do-Gooder, that marvelous but far from extinct specimen whose bite is frequently fatal and always noxious, has had a busy season. There is a lesson about all the self-conscious and self-assured Do-Gooders of the world in some recent stories about animals. At Chicago's Brookfield Zoo, for example, a group of Do-Gooders felt sorry for Ziggy, an elephant who got about in good health on a chain for dozens of years. How cruel, they cried, and promptly raised a fund to free him by building a moat around his area, in which he would now be able to walk free. The moat was dug, Ziggy was freed and promptly fell into the moat, scraping himself up badly and breaking his tusks. A classic triumph for the Do-Gooder.

And animal wardens in Upstate New York recently deprived two families of the young deer they had found ill on their farms and nursed back to good health, to the great delight of the children and neighbors. But the Do-Gooders, wearing government uniforms, insisted that living that way was bad for the animals. In the first case they hauled the animal away, only to have it die in the truck on the way to a supposedly safer pasture. In the second case they ended up shooting the animal as a solution.

Do-Gooders at work in both cases. So watch out for them; they are even harder on humans.

What can/can't be changed

The famous prayer of Alcoholics Anonymous asks for the help to change what can be changed and not to try to change what cannot be changed as well as the wisdom to know the difference. And here, of course, is something for everyone, a prayer easy to make our own even if we have never taken a drink in our lives. No little trouble comes from being mixed up on what can and what cannot be changed in our lives or in the lives of those around us.

What are some of the things we are likely to fail at changing? Each of us could make our own list, but we all might consider the following:

Our inheritance, both genetic and cultural. There is no way to change these even though we may transform our looks, our names, and our social level. For many years people trying to be successful were embarrassed to be anything but WASPs. Now, in the heyday of ethnic pride, the WASPs are getting apologetic for themselves.

Yet grim things happen to persons who disown such basic aspects of their personal identity. We cannot change our blood the way we change our car's oil. People who cut themselves off from their religious and national roots are the real poor of this world. They have thrown the symbols of their life history away and they can be remarkably empty and alienated as a result. To live against the grain of our own truth makes a cruel contradiction out of life.

Our friends. We can add here relatives, students, or any of the other people we have set our hearts on changing. We have very little luck trying to remake persons according to our own design for them, and we are wise when we do not invest too much energy in trying.

This is not to say that we should be disinterested in the

growth and development of others; it is to recognize that we should be committed to their growth rather than our ideas for their growth. How many tears and broken hearts the human race would be spared through understanding this.

Our limitations. What we do, if we are purposeful and lucky, is adjust to them and function well despite them. But we don't do very well by simply denying them. We get ourselves in trouble whenever we retouch our mind's-eye photo of ourselves to eliminate whatever is limited about us. In fact, this leads us to exaggerated expectations of our own performance because we hold out an impossible ideal for ourselves. And from this comes frustration and disappointment, much of it needless and all of it arising from thinking we can change something unchangeable about ourselves.

Our weaknesses. This is a special category of our limitations and it needs attention because we don't like to admit or look very closely at these. Our weaknesses may plague us for years; they won't completely go away but, as we become more mature, we handle them better. And we do this precisely because we understand that these weaknesses, even if we despise them, may abide. We handle them better after we have come to respect them, take them into account, and don't try to live as though they did not exist. We are stronger in the moment we develop a healthy respect for our weaknesses.

Our needs. Here is another category that we prefer to overlook or to deny altogether. We think it beneath us to have needs when actually it is only human. We need other persons, for example, even though we sometimes claim that we don't—or wish that we didn't.

We need people with whom we can be our true selves far more than we need powerful or influential acquaintances. We need to let ourselves be dependent in a healthy way at times, letting others care for us as one of the most mysterious and important of our human experiences. We need to be able to mourn and weep, to forgive and be forgiven, to let ourselves live fully and without denying our needs.

Our foibles. Include in this many of the experiences we wish we didn't have but which we go on having all the time. These include being distracted during church services; having wild, unbidden fantasies; and a host of highly individual flaws or imperfections of personality that are an important part of our identity.

Count in here the way we smile, hunch our shoulders, or the way we sound when we are most sincere. These are the elements of our individuality, the imperfections that make us charming rather than sinister, the scattered tiny treasures that people miss about us when we are away, the things that make us who we are.

Luckily, we are not too self-conscious about these things and so we are not tempted to change them. They are, in fact, evidence that we are unselfconscious, that we are free and unaffected even though we are never quite finished.

Things we can change

We have already wondered about some of the things that we cannot change; now it is time to flip the coin and explore those things we can change—the things before which we do not stand powerless, the modifications we can realistically make in ourselves and in our environment. These include, in only a partial listing, the following:

Our minds. It is a healthy thing to change our minds, not every day on every subject, of course, but regularly when we are wiser or have new information or have deepened our understanding of our human experience. It is not a bad thing to do because it is a sign that we are alive and responsive. Changing our minds on important matters means that our spirits are not fixed in cement; it goes along with greatness of soul as well as keenness of intellect. It is something to make life more interest-

ing, a transformation to make us safe from the circling vultures
of boredom.

Our direction.   Before we do this, of course, it is good to ask
what direction we're going in the first place. We may be idling
or quite still in the water, a slight tension on the anchor rope.
Some of us are just adrift, and at times we are all a little off
course. The worst thing that could happen would be to discover
that we have never left port. Most individuals living purposeful
lives, however, have a sense of direction that they neither inspect very often nor become very self-conscious about. They are
heading in the right direction, but it might reassure them to
inspect the evidence that proves this to them. This may consist
in the long lists of decisions made with integrity, of classes well
prepared and taught, of difficult situations faced honestly, of
emotional tangles worked through fully. If we have gotten this
far we will be able to believe more fully in ourselves in the
future.

Our ideals.   To entertain the idea of changing our ideals does
not mean that we are giving up on idealism or that we are abandoning the notion of making ourselves better. Changing our
ideals suggests that we are ready to modify our expectations,
perhaps in a more realistic fashion, because we now have a
deeper and more trustworthy knowledge of ourselves and our
capabilities. We revise our ideals only after we have a better
understanding of ourselves. People often fall short of attaining
their ideals because they have a poor sense of themselves. They
either overestimate or underestimate their abilities; such an in-
correct perception of the self doesn't do anybody any good.
Such persons fail in achieving their ideals or they have ideals
that don't really challenge them. We should not be afraid to
redraw the outlines of our ideals so that they are in better line
with the truth of our own selves.

Our style.   It is healthy for us to examine our typical pattern of
relationships with each other. What is the critical shape of it,
not the shape it has all the time? This might be too global an

outlook. Better to look at ourselves in tight times, when something is on the line, when there is something difficult to face or some truth to tell. What are we like then and could we be a little more open and straightforward, a little truer to what we really are? Sometimes we fall into a pattern of handling things rather than experiencing them, of learning to process events and people so that they do not bother us too much. Perhaps a certain amount of this is inevitable in life, but a refreshed life demands a reexamination of our style and an attempt always to make it a better reflection of the whole truth about ourselves.

Our schedule. This may be important for our physical and psychological health and, therefore, for our effectiveness in whatever work we are doing. We can begin by asking ourselves: What have I been doing to myself? Have I been treating myself fairly or have I at times ignored even the basic rules of good health? We don't have to make enormous changes in our schedules in order to improve them. Perhaps we can begin with a small effort to discover one thing that we can modify without losing much but gaining a lot at the same time. That might be as simple as a little extra sleep, a change in our food, or a change in the time and way we do some of our work.

Our understanding of life. We can always change this, not that we are going to adopt a new philosophy or religious tradition, but we are always able to go more deeply into existence and to discover more about the magic and contradictions of life itself. We change our understanding of life not by seeking a flashy new interpretation but by taking our own existence more seriously, by respecting ourselves enough to treat ourselves better than just a tourist's blurred-bus-window look of our own existence. This is an area we can do something about; in fact, it is an area *only* we can do something about.

What is luck?

Is it winning a lottery, turning the right corner at the right moment to bump into the person who will make all the difference in your life? Is it, in other words, a mysterious essence distilled in celestial realms but separate from us and our own abilities? And what about bad luck, which we usually describe as "just my luck"? Is that also an unkind visitor from another planet, an invisible but noxious ray directed at us by blind and unloving fate? Usually it is other people who get all the good luck while we are ones left not winning the lottery, not being noticed by the boss, and sometimes not seemingly getting anywhere either. Can we be bad-luck prone the way some people are accident prone? That seems to be a distinct possibility.

Perhaps this is why astrology is still so popular. Life is out of our hands according to its theories, and we can only hope that the planets and stars are aligned over us in the proper way; in any case, it is all written beforehand in the graphs and charts that we cannot alter. Letting things go as though our lives were really governed by mysterious forces outside us almost ensures that we will have bad luck. When we are passive in the face of life we almost guarantee bad fortune to ourselves. For passivity is linked to letting things go and not doing anything about them. If we think about the things we attribute to bad luck we may discover that they are not isolated incidents. The things we call bad luck are things that have happened to us before. Chances are that we are the ones who let them happen. It only seems like bad luck, like something outside of us even when it is a repeated pattern. That is why people who feel they are cursed by the fates use phrases like, It happens this way all the time!

Good luck belongs to people who do not just stand there and let life happen to them. They are active in response to it and to its difficulties. Taking a risk at the right moment in life is not the same as being reckless. Studies have shown that those persons who take well-timed risks double the advantage they have because they have skipped that phase of "waiting for something to turn up" or "waiting to see what happens." A person who opts for the latter course—an essentially passive stance—may find that things do get better. But it is also possible that things can get worse; by waiting, they have limited their capacity to respond. The person who takes the risk in time, however, not only gains the advantage of heading in a new direction but also does this well in advance of the long, slow turn of events by themselves. That is the way persons make good luck—by taking sensible risks, by using their abilities, by becoming active in their encounter with life.

It is also a commonplace observation that when we are in trouble we feel better if we do something. Our helplessness is only increased if we cannot respond or do not respond in any way at all. Becoming positive and active requires some renewal of our commitment, some willingness to take up our initiative once again. These are not only signs of life and health but they are the best guarantees we can have that the good luck we make will be our own.

CHAPTER 9

A time to rend and a time to sew
A time to be silent
and a time to speak . . .

Small talk

Americans may be the most communication conscious people on earth. Not only are they hooked by books that guarantee to interpret body language, photo analysis, and Freudian slips, but they are also quickly enlisted in any crusade to make communication "more meaningful." We are increasingly sensitive to hidden meanings and we are on a heavy trip for conversations that are weighted with significance. Some devotees of the profound would like us to be as quotable as Mao Tse-tung even in our casual conversations. It is a burden, always working ourselves up for supersincere communication with others.

We enjoy an evening at a good play or with a good book precisely because the conversation is so stimulating. The sparkling dialogue interlocks, the timing is just right, and none of the characters is plagued with the common human problem of discovering the right thing to say only long after the moment for saying it has passed. The arts condense and distort life, of course; nobody talks the way they do in plays by Shaw, Wilde, or even Neil Simon. We do not have a stock of bitingly humorous statements to deal with the difficulties of each day; most of us lack the energy needed to use vulgar language in the spectacular way that it is employed in many current films.

We class these things as escape entertainment. They take us

away from daily existence, allowing us to identify with the witty and the wise and helping us to forget our situation for a while. Nothing is as fiercely boring as parties at which the people attempt to act like characters in movies or films. Individuals who artificially strive to talk in throwaway lines—or who adopt ponderous philosophical tones or poses—are acting even though they are not on the stage. They do not talk to you; they lecture you. They are not interested in you; they are interested in your hearing about them and their opinions. They are hard to know; their identity is vague because they never say anything for themselves.

The truth that hurts

If we have ever had our casual moments—our small talk—taped we realize that most of us are not scintillating conversationalists. It is almost embarrassing to hear played back the fragmentary talk—as wild and unmatched as a random netting of migratory birds—that constitutes many of our irregular exchanges even with those closest to us. There are grunts, pauses, and strange and seemingly unrelated statements to which nobody pays any attention. Often it seems as though the people are not really listening to each other; they are just waiting, like cars at four-way stop signs, for their chance to go verbally. We would never think of ourselves as being coherent, much less grammatical, as we range across unconnected topics. A remarkable muddle, our small talk.

The remarkable thing, of course, is that we are able to communicate at all. If we survey the customary topics of our talks with each other we may discover that we tell the same anecdotes, make the same complaints, and even get into the same arguments with each other over and over again. Life can seem like a television rerun that we have seen many times before. Many of us would not mind if part of the tape of our lives was erased once in a while.

Pauses that refresh

We need a sustaining vision of life in order to support the small talk that is such a large part of it. Only some sensitivity to the fact that we live and communicate on levels deeper than the verbal saves us from suffocating in our own boredom. We live in the quiet spaces of life more than in the moments filled with noise. What we mean to each other as persons gives texture to our lives. It is only against that background that we can understand some of the mystery and meaning of the small talk that we exchange. As author Thornton Wilder has written, we have to "overhear" life if we are to grasp its deeper meanings.

Human beings have needs for escape, that is true, but they also need to step back periodically in order to examine their lives in better perspective. These pauses should be at peaceful moments aside from the enforced inspection that takes place at times of illness or crisis when we are suddenly confronted with what our lives signify and what we mean to each other. That is why we have birthdays and anniversaries, and why people never tire of hearing others tell them that they love them. It is even a good idea occasionally to step back—just as it is good to send a surprise card, a bouquet of flowers, or a small present— just for the hell of it.

Without these periodic long looks at ourselves, our days blur and dissolve into each other; we treat them as time to get through rather than to spend with one another. Many people, unaware of how they let themselves be cornered by their own lives, try to blot out any free moments with whatever distractions that are available. TV is perhaps the favorite form of making sure that there is no time for reflection or contemplation. Some people keep on the move, restlessly traveling from one source of artificial excitement to another. Little time is left when all the running is over; what do such persons do when they can run no longer? They may have killed time but they do not know themselves any better. They may have looked away from life's emptiness and its small talk. They are, however, no closer to grasping the inner experience that makes small talk and all the small things of life take on such a big meaning. They may have run so fast that they missed life altogether.

A time to pause

We can all profit by making more room in our lives for reflection on what is genuinely of value and on how we can continue to keep this in focus even when it seems always to be surrounded by the humdrum small talk and small deals of everyday life:

The pauses in life: There may be more of these than anything else, not only in our conversations but in our relationships with each other. Pauses are not the same as interruptions. They are quiet human times, and everybody needs them. Even the most blessed lovers are not talking to or even caressing each other all the time. Something is wrong if they are. In pauses, lovers listen to life together. During these periods when even small talk may be muted, something powerfully important takes place. During life's quiet moments people absorb their experience together, integrating it as part of themselves, allowing themselves to feel at a deeper level what they mean to each other. Such pauses are vital in all friendship and love. That is why friends can exchange small talk without boring each other. There is always something else going on, something richer and deeper between them that means that they are close enough to be quiet together.

Persons who are always talking may be afraid of these pauses. They are anxious because such pauses are truly interruptions for them, jagged rents in their defensive conversation which may reveal that they are not as substantial as they would like us to believe. Such pauses are empty periods for individuals who think that impressing and influencing others is at the heart of life.

Small events: These are frequently the ones that make us the happiest, the occasions that are not big deals and that cost little and yet remain imperishable treasures. When it is all counted up, the small things are the biggest signs of our affection for each other and of what we can really share with each other in life. Power decays, influence wanes, and fame is the most fickle goal of all; the treasures of small shared moments between people who love each other—they endure. Dr. Elisabeth Kübler-Ross has spoken of how dying patients survey their life and the moments they count in retrospect as important. "What they tell you are very tiny, almost insignificant moments in their lives—where they went fishing with a child or they tell of mountain-climbing trips in Switzerland. Some brief moments of privacy in an interpersonal relationship. These are the things that keep people going at the end. . . . They remember little moments that they have long forgotten and they suddenly have a smile on their faces. And they begin to reminisce about little memories that make their whole lives meaningful and worthwhile."

Perhaps it is at these moments—when we are unguarded because we trust each other—that we are able to touch each other's depths as truly as we are ever able to do it. At these times we need not impress each other and we can therefore simply and directly enjoy life with each other. These are never big events; such moments are the by-product always of purposeful relationships, the moments we discover when we truly give ourselves to love. Lovers can never lose these shared times and they are reassured by their memory that they have gotten beneath the surface of life. What else is worth remembering except that the smallest moments are finally the largest ones of all? Small talk takes on a new meaning in this perspective.

Ecstasy is in short supply. The very word means "to stand out from" our ordinary experience. This explains why some people seek excitement even in revolution or dangerous expeditions. Most of us are not redeemed by infrequent chances at ecstasy. We live without it, redeeming each other in the commonplace events that are built on the depths of what we really mean to each other. Joy is a small miracle built from a thousand seemingly insignificant exchanges, or uncounted moments of small talk and events that save us from the need for ecstasy.

We need time to remember that our most important gifts to each other are on a small scale. We cannot give to each other great treasures or celebrity. What we can give away we have in abundance—all those small occasions, small moments, and even small talk in which we can find and celebrate life together. We may have to empty ourselves of our own self-concern in order to see these better; we may need to surrender some of our own ease in order to make room for other people in our lives.

What story am I telling?

The reason conversations sometimes sound like juxtaposed monologues, with the participants yielding the floor only temporarily to each other, is that most of us are more interested in telling our story than we are in listening to somebody else's. We want to get something about ourselves and our experience across to someone else and we keep gamely at it even when hardly anybody listens.

We are somewhat like ham radio operators sending out our messages into the night, our reward resting in their being received by someone—and anyone will do—somewhere out there. We are not whole until someone receives us, until someone validates our existence by accepting it with understanding into their own. That is a basic process in the task of being human. We want somebody to hear us as we tell the story of our lives. The question becomes: Do we hear ourselves at all? Do we understand the kind of story we are telling to the world all the time?

Those seeking self-understanding can profit more from listening to themselves than from most of the gurus who promise to deliver wisdom and peace these days. It is amazing that we can be engaged in telling people about our life and not pay too much attention to it ourselves. But that is what we are up to, the very thing we are waiting to get a chance to do.

Some of us tell sad stories and some tell happy ones; some of us never get past the beginning, like a writer stuck for a good lead, or because we like the beginning better than anything that has happened since. Others tell science fiction tales of things they have not done but that they plan to do, of plans spun far out into the future, well beyond the limits of the present. Some tell a story they wish were true, while still others tell of things they would have done if only they had the breaks, or if things had been different. . . . But we all tell a story, and to under-

stand ourselves we should begin listening to what we are saying.

Not logically . . .

Well, not exactly to what we are saying. We don't tell the story
of our lives neatly or logically. It is made up of loose ends,
unfinished sentences, and a few sighs here and there. In Thornton Wilder's phrase again, we have to "overhear" ourselves and
not just record every word we speak.

As nature is liberal with its seedlings, so we overproduce,
generating more material than we need to get our meaning
across. This is why we repeat so much or use so many examples
to say the same kind of thing. We must pause and be quiet to
catch the point of our own stories, to grasp the reason we tell
them in the first place. What is it that we are trying to get across
anyway? And why are we taking such a long time to do it?

Identifying the theme of our story is the first step in using our
daily conversations as a source of self-discovery. We can tap
into that by asking ourselves, What am I feeling in order to be
saying these things? What, in other words, is the point of the
examples we pile up; what is the tone of our tale?

We may tell an angry story that projects our frustration at
whatever trap we feel we are in and not really hear what we are
saying. Or it may be a gentle story of self-acceptance and con-
tentment whose theme is compassion more than anything else.

Whatever it is, we can be sure that we are always sending out
revealing messages about ourselves and that we can hear them if
we take the time to listen. Self-knowledge does not come so
much from the stories other people tell us as it does from the
story of our own days, one we are always narrating, and one we
can tune in to more carefully anytime we choose.

Indulging others (and ourselves)

The last shred of truth is precious and, at all costs, must be
exhumed. That, in an era of romantic investigative reporting,
congressional inquiries, and supposedly psychotherapeutic con-

frontations, is what we hold dear in America these days. But is it right? And is it even wise? Would the world end if we did not know the last detail, sordid or not, about John F. Kennedy, Richard Nixon, or even ourselves?

There is something to be said for *not* getting to the bottom of things, at least not of all things. Life would stiffen and crumble away under the assaults on privacy and the revelations that would have to be made in order to expose the truths of all hearts to a restlessly curious world. The question becomes: Aren't some things better left unsaid and unreported?

The truth of a person's life cannot, in the end, be reduced to one cruel or salacious anecdote. The real truth is in the whole shape of our lives and is neither decreased nor increased much by little stories about our smallest oddities or most minute virtues. Our lives are viewed as the average of our best intentions and most loving accomplishments. The trivial footnotes about our failings never tell the story at all.

Besides, could life be lived if there were no margin for error, if we could never make a mistake that others were not ready to overlook, if not to forget completely? Could society survive long if we had to own up to our least gracious moments with the prospect of neither pardon nor peace for our imperfect state?

The truth is, of course, that life is not lived well by insisting on the whole truth from everybody. We manage our way through it on the grace notes given by those who choose to be understanding enough to take our humanity into consideration and not charge us for it. To be understanding involves our willingness to look deeply into each other, ignoring much of what is half-finished or otherwise imperfectly wrought. Understanding is not soft when it passes over weakness and does not make a liar out of somebody over a matter that does not amount to very much.

Ruthlessness digs out the truth and doesn't know what to do with it except to hurt or startle, neither of which advances us in the ways of wisdom. The "public's right to know" is invoked. But loving people thrive not by insisting on their rights as much as by knowing when to forgo them out of sensitivity to each other. Neither marriage nor friendship—and maybe not even society—can survive on brutalized truths about persons that may have no relation to the whole truth of their lives.

We all need to be indulged a little by those who put up with our foibles, allow us to ramble on with the same old stories, or exaggerate our past accomplishments. We need somebody gentle enough not to insist that we tell the truth, the whole truth, and nothing but the truth about our failures or our regrets. A lot of such understanding goes into raising a child, keeping a friend, or deepening a marriage.

A remarkable thing frequently happens when we know a person who is willing to let us get by without making us feel wretched by tearing away the gauzy disguise of our fictional defense. When we have a little time we ordinarily set the record straight ourselves; we get things into better perspective on our own and we correct our own tall tales or lame excuses. But the truth remains hidden when somebody is too insistent on tearing it out of us. Perhaps it is worth thinking about in this day of holding nothing back. We have lost something precious about our sense of ourselves in insisting that every shameful souvenir of our poor lives should be excavated. Only the truth that is compounded of gentleness and compassion really sets us free.

Don't say it

What is the most helpful rule of thumb for a happy life? Try this one: When in doubt, don't say it! As a matter of fact, half the time it is a good idea not to say it even if you're not in doubt.

This advice has particular relevance to relationships with close friends whom we would like to keep that way; neighbors even if they are ordinarily vague, somewhat distant presences; and any and all relatives. Why? Because the actions of these people usually tempt us to say impulsive things that can do nothing but cause ongoing trouble.

We are tempted in regard to these people because we get to know their foibles and their habits. Sometimes we are even convinced that although it goes unnoticed by the unobservant or indifferent world, the evidence we have gathered on them could get them put away for good.

And this is what irritates us so much and moves us, like nations edging toward nuclear conflict, ever closer to telling them off. It can be something as irritating as a neighbor who has a habit of ignoring your property line in small ways. Or it can be the way certain relatives raise—or don't seem to care about raising—their children. It can be a character flaw, ever so small, in a dear friend. Any or all of these may cause us to vow under our breath that someday, yes, someday we are going to tell them off about this nagging concern.

Well, justified though you must be, don't say it. Don't tell your in-laws what has bugged you about the way they blow on their hot soup; don't tell a cherished friend that his favorite anecdote has been told too often; don't tell brothers, sisters, or cousins of any kind the tiny things that have bothered you about them over the years. And forget about reforming your neighbor, who, like all the rest of these people, will feel that whatever problem you bring up is your own fault anyway.

The problem here is that telling people about their abrasive eccentricities does not do any good. It does not solve the problem; it just gets them mad at you, sometimes permanently.

Very few people want constructive advice about their behavior even though they may say things like, "I really want you to tell me the truth about this." Hardly anybody ever means that; moreover, as sure as not, the things that irritate us so much are the very kinds of things we are probably doing to irritate other people.

We all have loose ends that other people notice and manage not to mention. Benignly overlooking is one of the ways we manage to survive as a race. When something small begins to irritate us excessively we are better off trying to understand why we are so touchy about this individual issue than we are in stalking the streets, *High Noon* fashion, for vengeance. Wisdom comes from finding such things out. And so, too, does a life that is less frenzied and more tolerant.

One hardly needs to add that these things are vital during the vacation season, when the best of families and friends can have stupendous fallings-out over the funny things they find out about each other at close range.

What do you say to somebody who . . .

It is all very well to put up with our respective rough edges, you say, but what about real problems? Perhaps there is no more common question after lectures than this type: What do you say to somebody you live with when you think she or he is going down the wrong path? What do you say to a spouse who suddenly seems different to you?

The questions are not small ones; neither is their motivation mere curiosity. These are the queries of concerned persons who want to be of assistance to other individuals. The only answer I have ever been able to give centers on the constructions of such questions.

Is our problem really finding out *what to say* to others? When this concern enters our souls it may be a signal to begin *to listen* more actively than we have to the other, whether it is a student, a friend, or a family member. Have we really heard them, heard their total message, that is, and made room enough for them in our lives?

The urge to preach to or straighten out others is far more common than our readiness to hear what they are trying to tell us about themselves, sometimes in symbols and sometimes in words. It is remarkable what happens when we resist the impulse *to say* something to others and begin *to hear* what they have to say for themselves.

When we listen, whether it is to a wondering youth or a seemingly wandering friend, we make it possible for them to hear themselves again. We provide anchor points that help them stabilize themselves and their existence long enough to regain their balance completely. We all need time and space to discover the meaning of our own conflicts; and we also require good friends around us to take our soundings as we seek a surer path.

What else can we really give each other in life? Advice is cheap, repetitive, and largely unheeded. Actively listening to the person we want to say something to (always "for their own good," of course) is not a small gift. It is the gift of a richer life. And you get it back in the very moment that you give it away.

Eyes

As far as the person is concerned, the eyes indeed have it. Swiftly and subtly they register our moods and our longings. Their light—sometimes as fierce as the afternoon sun—reflects our anger and—sometimes as soft as evening shadow—our love and tenderness too. "An eye for an eye," the Old Testament cried, and from the hearts of the vengeful, spring looks black and sharp enough to kill. We speak of the mind's eye and the eyes of faith, and we know of the eyes that are unable to see the world's beauty as well as eyes that are blinded in the way hearts are hardened.

It is not surprising that the eyes should be such a sensitive source of medical diagnosis. They give hints of what is going on in the central nervous system as accurately as they tell of what is going on in our hearts. Our eyes reflect our general well-being, and the knowing physician peers like a miner into them for the tiniest clues about our health. It is striking that the eyes, perhaps more than any other part of us, resist disguise. We are vulnerable in our eyes because we cannot easily conceal all that they say about us and our lives. You cannot hide a bright eye any more than you can successfully alter the effects of too much drugs on the size of its pupil. You can tell when you are being looked at by eyes that violate your privacy. And you cannot hide a lack of comprehension in eyes that stare but neither see nor understand what is in their view. Neither is there anything more beautiful than a lover's glance, nor as touching as a tear pumped out of a lonely heart.

Respect may be what gangster godfathers crave, but as a word, its roots tell us that it means a special way of looking at other persons, a way, as one dictionary has it, "of not violating them." Lovers create an open space with their glances in which they can stand together freely and safely. The depths of love may be seen in the meeting of lovers' eyes, the kind of eyes that the poet Byron thought were souls themselves.

Our entire human story may be read in the eyes around us. We can see our possibilities in the trusting glance of a child; there is a special majesty in the wonder-filled eyes of parents as they look at their newborn child for the first time; joy is found in the crinkled eyes of people who remember how to laugh at themselves even in the midst of life's most severe pressures. And fear, like a dark wind on a pond, changes our eyes in an instant; sometimes it clouds our eyes for years after a damaging experience. You can see that fear still in the eyes of survivors of some of the terrible events of our century.

There are also eyes that have seen everything and have managed somehow both to forgive and redeem the world for all its faulted beauty. Such are the eyes of those who keep looking at life without blinking or backing away from it. There is a quiet wisdom, a peace that passes understanding, in the eyes of persons who have maturely come to terms with life.

The person is there

The eyes which reveal so much are also the subject of entire industries that attempt to transform or hide their messages. Eye makeup goes back beyond the royal Egyptians, while dark glasses have always provided a double benefit: protection from the sun and a form of disguise. They hide people better than false beards precisely because they cover the very part of us that defines us so clearly to each other. Hide a person's eyes and he or she is hard to find. There is nothing as frustrating as not being able to see the look in another person's eyes when we are trying to understand him.

We are familiar with the experts who try to teach us how to speak more effectively in public. They make much of "eye contact," even offering tricks to be employed by the speaker or the salesman so that he can seem to be looking into another person's eyes even when this is not the case. Such interpersonal strategists suggest, for example, that the individual who wants to project sincerity should focus on the bridge of the other's nose rather than directly into the other's eyes. The reason for this is simple: you could hardly sustain phony sincerity if you looked straight into the eyes of another. Eye contact must be avoided in the name of achieving simulated eye contact. It is one of our contemporary bits of logic, something like bombing a city in order to save it from destruction.

Faking the meeting of our eyes with those of others is doomed, of course, to failure. We cannot carry on that kind of deception for very long, and we are bound in many other ways to betray the phoniness that goes along with such stylized efforts at sincerity. We are present in our eyes far more clearly than in our clothing or in the words we may choose to speak. There is no long-term, successful way by which we can hide the truths that our eyes communicate. It is no accident that at serious moments in life, we automatically look into each other's eyes both as a sign and a guarantee of our interest and concern for each other. It is also true that when we cannot face some twisted event or hurt—or when we are trying to hide something —we do not feel much like looking into each other's eyes. It is a test as ancient as friendship, a still lively moment of truth in which we clearly show whether we are as open and authentic as we claim to be.

What does it mean to be open?

Openness has been a key word during the last decade. Be open, our neighbors, friends, and family insist—be open, the professionals and book writers tell us—be open and you will find your life and save your soul. What does openness lead to? Certainly openness is an attractive idea, yet although it can mean so much, it may, if we are not careful, end up meaning very little. If openness is the ideal of the age and a valid goal, it is something we want to understand in depth. And we all know that there seems to be something in us that wants, at times, at least, to close down and cover up, to hide away from the world and all its demands. The beginning of a new year is traditionally the time for resolutions, for focusing on the specific practices or virtues we wish to make our own, for ironing out the unruly spots in our psyches. Perhaps, instead of making many specific resolutions, it would be more profitable to think of some general resolution, something connected with our own openness to life and to each other.

Specific resolutions are a great hazard, especially for obsessive persons who tend to drive themselves and everyone else a little crazy in trying to carry them out to perfection. Highly individualized resolutions make us concentrate on our actions more than on our underlying attitudes. This is what the behavioral school of psychology recommends as an effective way of modifying ourselves. However, wisdom that has survived centuries of history bids us look at ourselves in general rather than just at our particular actions.

Frequently what needs modification or development is our attitude toward life and toward ourselves and those close to us. This is where being open may be a significant source of contemplation for each of us. There may be many things we want to change about ourselves, but for this year at least, it may be appropriate to think about only one general aspect of our personality. If we can make some small transformation in this area, countless other changes will occur without our thinking about them. That is the way growth manifests itself when it flows from something sound, healthy, and enduring. It is the best way to grow, slowly and from the inside; this kind of growth cannot be taken away from us by a shattered resolution or by a single failure. It is the deep kind of growth that carries us over our small misfortunes and rescues us from our constant foibles. If we make ourselves just a little more open to life and to persons around us, we will be graced with the best of blessings, with peace and joy and deepened love.

Openness means

There is nothing very complicated about openness. The endless talk about it makes it seem more difficult to achieve than it really is. One of the characteristics of the open individual, for example, is that he or she can see things as they are rather than as they are expected to be. Open persons respect individuality and the qualities that inhere in persons or events rather than those we impose from outside. To be able to see things in this way has remarkable consequences both for ourselves and for those around us.

Such openness enables us to see things freshly, as always newborn and filled with possibilities. Such an outlook is the antidote to cynicism and bitterness, those twin plagues of closed-off persons. This style of openness to what others can become is also an essential ingredient of belief in them. Such openness, in other words, enables us to see persons as individuals rather than as categories or groups or, as sometimes happens, as threatening mobs. It also enables us to see the totality of the other person, rather than just some feature that distracts or annoys us. At times we look at the world around us with the eye of the caricaturist, quickly focusing on flaws and missing the strong and attractive qualities in others. Being open means we are able to see beyond appearances because we are accustomed to looking deeply and with compassion into the lives of others.

This is the openness husbands and wives and friends everywhere need in order to keep their relationships alive and loving. People who are with each other a great deal can get tired of each other. They can feel that they have learned everything there is to know about the other and then close themselves off from ever learning or hearing anything new. It is no wonder that so many friendships and marriages die; the partners in them have long since given up on the openness required for a fresh view of each other every day. Real lovers are making friends with each other anew all the time.

Nothing is sadder than persons who only remember their love, whose essential attitude toward it is one of mourning because they can merely remember it and know that it is now dead. Openness is our response to that; it is a source of renewal because it makes it possible for friends always to see and appreciate more about each other. It never closes the books or writes the final comment; that is why people who truly love each other keep growing with each other and never get so out of step that they can only look back at what they once shared but can no longer reclaim.

Moods

We live in a cloud of moods all the time, but what do they tell us? What can we learn from them? They are passing phenomena, one school holds, and are untrustworthy and generally to be ignored or dismissed by a spasm of the will. Others, however, see moods as special messages filled with power and meaning and feel that we are diminished if we do not pay attention to them.

And we know of the drugs described as mood changing, just as we recognize the popularity of mood rings as small reflections of personality, worth the price even if they are more show business than mystery. We know our own moods, and people tell us about them if we do not pay enough attention. "You're in a bad mood today!" a friend will say, startling us at times with this perception. Byron thought that the soul took wing in a mood; it certainly can take shape in one, good or bad, craggy or smooth.

Our moods hang like mist about us, offering testimony to the truth of our personhood and of our values. The mood reveals us even when we strive to conceal ourselves; it is like an aura, a zone of the spirit that tells whether we are at peace or in conflict, whether we are loved or lonely, whether we live in a deep or shallow manner.

A flight from feeling

This is the diagnosis offered compassionately by psychoanalyst Herbert Hendin in his book *The Age of Sensation*. Reporting on his extensive research with young people who are, Hendin believes, afraid of genuine emotional involvement, he writes: "The students I saw tried many escape routes. The main one moved in two seemingly different directions: One toward numbness and limited, controlled experience; the other toward impulsive action and fragmented sensory stimulation." Sometimes, Dr. Hendin says, the same person will try both paths. The goal is "to perform, but not to feel, to acquire sensory experiences without emotional involvement" so as not to understand or to acknowledge a person's own true feelings.

Many members of the younger generation have expectations of life that are quite different from those of their parents. They "see emotional involvement as the surest route to disaster, and . . . fragmentation or detachment as the best means of survival." What is fragmentation, according to Dr. Hendin? Its essence, he writes, lies in a "sense of life and relationships as a succession of experiences without meaning or purpose . . . the means of concealing their own feelings and avoiding the emotions of others and of eliminating intimacy in friendship or sex."

Dr. Hendin feels that Kurt Vonnegut has become a cultural hero to this generation because he "captures in a wildly imaginative way their daily ironies, problems, and solutions." Thus Billy Pilgrim in *Slaughterhouse Five* learns the value of detachment. The Tralfamadorians teach Billy the astral point of view. They have "wars as horrible as any you've ever seen or read about. There isn't anything we can do about them, so we simply don't look at them. We ignore them. We spend eternity looking at pleasant moments—like today at the zoo. Isn't this a nice moment?" Dr. Hendin feels that these fictional characters offer youth a distanced way to deal with loss as well. For people only appear to die. "When a Tralfamadore sees a corpse, all he thinks is that the dead person is in bad condition in that particular moment, but that the same person is just fine in plenty of other moments." So Billy can shrug now when he hears that someone has died and say, "So it goes."

One need not agree totally with Dr. Hendin's analysis to be stimulated to think deeply about the mood of youth and its implications for all persons concerned with human and religious values.

A mood is a sign of what Dylan Thomas described as "the weather of the heart." It is a measure of our presence in life, a tone true as that of a great bell that identifies us. The mood of some persons is like sunlight, while that of others is mostly shade and we are warmed or chilled by them. Perhaps the majority of us have moods like summer days—clouds and sun with a chance of afternoon thundershowers.

Our moods are powerful because through them we not only express ourselves but we also produce some of our deepest effects on others. Mood is a medium through which we communicate the things that make all the difference in life, the distillates of the soul like trust and tenderness that strengthen and enlarge those around us. Norman Mailer comments on one of Martin Buber's *Tales of the Hasidim* in which a man rushing to put out a fire in his barn is calmed by a visiting rabbi. The fire goes out as the man's mood changes from anxiety to peacefulness. Mailer remarks: "When the Hasid pauses to listen to the speech of the rabbi, he is in effect ready to relinquish his wealth. So what has been evil in him expires, and what has been heat for the flame in the grain is now cooled." He goes on to ask: "Is it not as plausible to assume we have a spirit which is communicable to other people and other properties of our environment as it is to assume that spirit does not exist and is not communicable? And is it not equally comfortable to assume that a fire may be extinguished by a dramatic shift in mood? Let the burden fall on the philosopher who would prove that the existence of a fire can never be affected by a mood" *(Cannibals and Christians,* The Dial Press, 1966).

Does the poetic insight go too far? Or is there more truth about the meaning and power of mood here than there is in the numerical scales of a psychological test? We generate our moods in our innermost souls. How can they fail to have power? How can they fail to affect our environment? What happens when someone we love comes to us at a time of trouble and changes the mood of our lives with a gift of peace? The day is less dark, the atmosphere is lightened, and we are in some way different, healed by another's spirit.

Watch a room change according to the moods of those who inhabit it. Are the woods warmer in the presence of friends? Is a church different because of the mood—because of the state of the soul of the minister? One cannot doubt it. A church is as spirited as its clergyman—cramped and mean as an airport waiting room when he is distracted and in a hurry, but filled with easy space and a feeling of faith when he possesses his own soul. Houses have moods because of the people who live in them, and schools have them because of the people who teach in them.

Our moods are an example of everyday mysticism. They fit the undramatic but powerful nature of the religious edging of everything that seems commonplace in our existence. God does not work great signs in the skies for most of us; he touches us in and through the human responses that seem small only to those with a poor sense of measurement.

Splitting

Perhaps this mood of noninvolvement is one of the factors responsible for the widespread phenomenon of persons "living together" rather than getting married. They can get out, in accord with the freedom implicit in such arrangements, when they no longer meet each other's needs. They don't divorce, they "split." And splitting is a new kind of divorce that has been talked and written about extensively of late. Splitting is becoming institutionalized; lawyers are involving themselves, and some cases have been won by women against men with whom they had lived for a number of years. And, oh yes, people are beginning to write of the emotional cost of just splitting, of how, in fact, this has not healed all the emotional wounds of old-fashioned divorces.

What does it mean if not that something catches up with human beings, something deeply rooted in them that longs for something more stable than relationships that are kept tentative in order to protect the hearts of those involved in them. But love comes fully to those who expose their hearts, who make a commitment for all to see, who take the chance of everything going wrong in order to have something central and important in life come right.

One must wonder at the seeds of longing that are growing beneath the adjustments so many people make in order to keep themselves from emotional hurt. How will it all seem ten years from now, and how then will it seem to the children, if there are children? What, in other words, will be the price of the present restricted emotional involvement as it is paid by people in the future? Will love be even harder and seem more than ever a stroke of fate or luck? Will sensation—feeling without commitment—finally have spent its energies because of its failed promise?

What can ordinary persons give to the world? Not the least of the gifts of those who will never be famous is the simple sense of how to live deeply and lovingly. It is a simple donation to the present and the future, the very thing, in fact, that the world, worn down and weary, needs more than any other. This is given to the world without ceremony and through the very act of living itself. It is bestowed every time human beings open their hearts without qualification to each other. It is a gift found in every gentle revelation of truth between those who love each other. It is the everyday gift that defeats time and delivers to us a taste of eternity.

The poetry of life

Some people grow up with a prejudice against poetry. It probably goes back to their early school days, when, against their will and inclination, they had to memorize rhymes that, they were told, were great poetry. Poetry forced on people at too early an age is as dangerous as anything else given to individuals before they are ready to absorb or understand it. But life would be a hardscrabble place, a ghost town at best, if we were deprived of a poetic sense and cut off from feeling the awful grandeur of being alive.

Poetry has never been well defined. Poems, in a way, are the least of it; they are end products, glowing fragments—but only fragments—from the visions of our most sensitive human beings. They tell, in part, that the whole of life is filled with poetry, with illuminating moments and extraordinary people and places charged with the magic of existence. Every experience perceived by a poet defines for us some portion of the dappled mystery of our existence. We may have to give up the American habit of hurrying in order to see everything that is poetic and therefore profoundly religious in life all around us.

Maybe in hard times we need poetry more than ever. Anytime, of course, is a good time for glimpsing the everyday revelations that deliver to us a sense of the meaning of our lives. But autumn may be the best season for poetry because it is a season of constant change. It has been observed that although there is midwinter and midsummer, there is neither midspring or midautumn. Neither of these seasons pauses; they move on, like life, constantly unfolding their mysteries to us.

The English novelist and poet Thomas Hardy once wrote, "Give me the roughest of spring days rather than the loveliest of autumn days for there is death in the air." This is precisely why the long fall teems with revelation. We need to taste autumn's ripened fruit even as we despair of holding on to the last days of the beautiful summer.

Fall is the time of mystery that returns as silent and sure as the tide. It sweeps us and confronts us steadily with the inevitabilities of the human situation: that we must age, that life is filled with greetings and good-byes, with closeness and loneliness, with the recurrent rhythm of separation and death.

Fall is a time for reflection, because unless we face the mystery of change that it acts out for us we would understand neither the sleep of winter nor the resurrection of spring. But you have to look at autumn, walk through it and feel it even when it is bittersweet in your bones. It is a season for all men and women, and in its clear and crisp air we can see the poetry of our existence more clearly.

Poetic places

One summer I stood in an exact restoration of a fort that was used as a trading post by Canadian fur companies three hundred years ago. Standing with sympathetic and silent companions, I looked through the imperfect glass of the old windows and I could see an edge of the stockade, part of the forest, and the blue sky beyond. I realized that this was exactly what some other person, standing in this spot, looked at hundreds of years before. There was no intrusion of jet trails, television antennas, or telephone cables. One could not view this quiet scene without feeling history in a new way; one understood in greater depth all those who have gone before us with whom we have shared the same seas and skies. One could not gaze out this window without having a greater feeling of tenderness for all those who have preceded us, for all their joys and sadnesses, for all the feelings that we surely share in common with them. Standing in such a place renews one's readiness to be patient with all those with whom we now share life.

Or take a railroad station, as author John Cheever does, and see it not as an out-of-date building but as a human symbol, striking architectural poetry about our passages together. In a short story in *The World of Apples* (Warner Paperback Library, 1974, p. 97), Cheever writes as a man recalling his wait for an overdue train at the Union Station in Indianapolis: "The station there—proportioned like a cathedral and lit by a rose window—is a gloomy and brilliant example of that genre of architecture that means to express the mystery of travel and separation. The colors of the rose window, limpid as a kaleidoscope, dyed the marble halls and the waiting passengers. A woman with a shopping bag stood in a panel of lavender. An old man slept in a pool of yellow light."

We suddenly realize why old train stations were built to resemble churches, with an atmosphere of great distances, and new-styled seats in which to wait and wonder. It is a place of our comings and goings, of our good-byes and our returns. Anything that witnesses that much of human affairs is necessarily religious if we can but see it in the right light. There is a lot of us—of our human poetry—in such a location. There is indeed something sacred about the places where we part and the places where we come together again after long and separate journeys. They are points of mystery, crossroads and terminals at which we can sense the things we value and the strength of our commitments to each other.

We could use more poetry in the design of our airports. For that matter, we could use more of it in the design of some modern churches that, if anything, are imitating what is worst in airports in their ribs of cold and angular chrome, and their lack of comfortable places in which to wait and think. The modern sacrilege is to take a chair and build a coin-operated TV set on its arm to keep travelers from noticing any of the human poetry around them. In our places of comings and goings there is always more than a hint of eternity.

What do we learn while we sit and wait that we could learn in no other way? There is, in fact, a sense of promise that overcomes the sadness of the platforms where we say farewell. And nothing surpasses the joy of the moment of return after a long absence. These feelings open a window for us on the mystery of the journey we share across the seasons of existence together. If we hurry through autumn the way we hurry through airports, we may miss the wonder in things that surround us all the time.

A lesson from lovers

Observe, if you will, people who love each other. We are all inspired by young lovers who have just discovered each other and who are so filled with dreams and plans. We even envy them a little, at least their youth and their readiness to start again the pilgrimage into mystery that goes with sharing life with somebody else. But look also at people who have been friends for a longer time, at people who have stayed in love across the years. They may no longer be youthful; an acquired peace and certainty may have supplanted the enthusiasms and starry-eyed qualities of an earlier time. There is, however, poetry here, a sense of depth, of promises kept, wounds healed, and the extraordinary and unmistakable power that emanates from people who have worked through a thousand problems and stayed in touch with each other. All the poetry of life speaks to us when we are blessed enough to be with those who have remained themselves and yet have plumbed deeply the mystery of sharing life.

Lovers, old or young, renew us. They teach us something, enriching us and making us think again of ourselves and of the opportunities we may still use to be more loving and true in our own lives. It is not surprising that author Joseph Epstein, in his book *Divorced in America: An Anatomy of Loneliness* (E. P. Dutton &

Co., Inc., 1974), should write the following: "Good marriages will depend even more than they do now, on selflessness, character and love. They could well become our rarest work of art." And like great works of art everywhere, lovers speak to us of timeless truths, of the meaning of faithfulness, and of the willingness to understand and forgive that keeps us and love alive.

Have you listened to yourself?

Almost all of us want to know about ourselves. We are all at least secretly fascinated with our personalities. The strange thing, however, is that when we want to find out about ourselves we often ask somebody else. This is doubly peculiar when we think of the amount of time we can spend talking about ourselves—for some people, every chance they get. In the pursuit of self-understanding, however, it seems to never occur to some people to listen to themselves.

Instead they turn from one expert to another. We have had a rash of perfect masters ready to take in disciples to show them some way, newly paved in gold, to peace and self-possession. The astrologers are still doing a good business with their vague directions about, "It's a good day to make new friends but do not forget old ones," and the like. Some people still like to have their tea leaves read, while others try to discover themselves in a more segmented form, as though they were putting themselves together like the Six Million Dollar Man. They turn, for example, from a book on willpower to a book on memory to a book on how to control their blood pressure through biofeedback. They are literally trying to get it all together. If somebody wrote a book entitled *Thirty Days to a Healthier Gallbladder*, it would probably sell in the millions.

We don't have to seek ourselves in the stars, or in the leavings in our teacups, or in the various perfectible sections of our personality. All we have to do, if we truly want to grow more deeply in self-understanding, is listen to ourselves. We are, in one way or another, always talking to ourselves, so it is not as difficult as it first seems. Add to that a little gentle watching of ourselves and we can increase our self-knowledge immensely.

Listening to ourselves—like telling the truth for some politicians—seems like either the last resort or a secret weapon; this is not surprising. Many people look away from themselves or do not trust themselves. They have no idea of how to look beneath their feelings or to interpret the various signals that come, as clear as the white smoke of a papal election, from their behavior all the time. The problem, you see, is not that we are hiding things from ourselves. It is rather that we are not looking or listening.

What do we listen to?

We can begin our adventures in hearing ourselves in a very simple way. We can listen to the way we spend each day. Some persons don't spend the day as much as they kill it or slowly strangle it to death. They are always waiting for something that is going to happen after they get finished doing what lies before them, whether that is schoolwork, their job, or a conversation with somebody else. And when they get through they may not be quite able to remember what they were waiting to do. Evening comes, they take off their shoes and they are at last alone. They have survived the day. What does it mean to live holding oneself back ever so slightly from one's work or one's play? Would boredom be a surprising visitor in such a life?

Other people, if they listen and watch themselves a little more closely, may discover that they spend most of each day waiting for various events to occur. They wait for breakfast to be served, for example, and then for the news to come on the radio or television. They wait then for the paper and after that for the mail. They wait for a coffee break or lunch, for the ball game to begin, the evening news, dinner, and, at a last familiar outpost for many Americans, they wait for the final weather forecast of the day. One wonders why. They are not going anyplace. They manage to get through the hours not really expecting anything but making their way, like someone climbing hand over hand up a long ladder, through the vague terrain of each day.

Neither of these kinds of people is very alive. They are living suspended existences. Self-revelation could only break them open to a more lively sense of their own presence and to a richer feeling for the gift of their own existence. They are missing life and they can only find it if they begin to ask themselves why they are staying on the outside of things.

What is the pattern?

Much livelier people than these can still catch a pattern or shape that may previously have eluded them by listening carefully to themselves. What we talk about, the behavior we engage in, the priorities we set—these reflect our beliefs and our values. They tell who we are. What are some of the more specific areas to which we can give our attention?

How do we listen to people? What attitude, in other words, do we manifest in the way we receive and make room for others in our lives? This tells a great deal about our approach to ourselves and, perhaps better than anything else, lets us know whether we lead lives of self-containment or genuine sharing.

Do we, for example, always find ourselves judging others, sorting them out as good or bad, interesting or dull, according to our own whims or inclinations? Or do we perceive others as at least mildly threatening? They may come too close or take over our privacy, and so we use strategies to keep them at a distance or on the very surface of our lives. Do we look at people as persons in themselves or as problems that have to be handled? We may complain about being lonely at times and, only as we watch ourselves handle others, discover that we have a hand in maintaining our own isolation.

What are the things we do first? This does reveal quite clearly our priorities. It tells us operationally what we believe in because it rides point on the activities of the day. The things we do first reflect clearly the elements that are most significant in our picture of ourselves. We may be tempted to deny it when we look at the evidence of the activities to which we give our best energies. There is, however, no way of looking successfully away from the evidence. What gets our first attention says something quite clearly about ourselves.

What are the things we do last? This is the lower bracket of our set of values, the things that can be postponed or that we do not feel much like doing, or the things, in other words, that we value least of all. These can include a number of activities that are not minor in themselves but that we have pushed to the edges of our life space.

What are the things we never quite get done at all? These are easy to find because we are always saying, "I've been meaning to get around to that," or "I'm going to do something about this someday. . . ." We may not have to look very deeply to discover the reasons we postpone or put off things. The signals are often very clear; we can, for example, recognize that we may always strive to avoid potential conflicts—or dealing with certain persons—or straightening out certain aspects of our own lives. We are the ones who do that. These things don't happen to us, and as we come closer to them, we can understand ourselves much better.

What are the things we would make sacrifices for? What, in other words, are the activities we would give up sleep, time, or privacy in order to accomplish? The nature of these tells something about our values and the nature of our personal characters. There are certain things that are never too much trouble for us to do but there is a whole other class of things that are always too much trouble. In between these lies the truth about ourselves.

Who is the one we let pay for our own lateness or delays? We can only find the answer to this question if we are able to look at the pattern of the way we handle the events of our lives. We may discover that although it is our own poor planning or lack of attention that gets us into a certain situation, we expect somebody else to pay our way out. There is, for example, the person whose rights we are ready to step on because we know that we can get away with it. There may be those whose appointments are the first ones to be canceled if an emergency arises; there may be persons we inconvenience because we feel that we can get away with it at the least expensive emotional cost. If these turn out always to be the same person, this tells us something about ourselves and our way of relating that we can learn in no other way.

How do we see ourselves? That is the old question of the Scottish poet who hoped for the gift of seeing himself in the same way that others did. This seems difficult, however, especially if we never listen to or watch what we actually do with our lives.

I am reminded of an old friend with whom I had dinner not too many years ago. I had not seen him in some time, and when he arrived, I noticed that his appearance had been notably changed because he was wearing a jet black wig. He seemed calm and self-assured, however, but my eyes were drawn to it as a willing subject's are to a trinket dangled by a hypnotist trying to induce a trance. We sat at dinner, and although I tried to look out a window or at other people in the restaurant my eyes kept fixing directly at the new wig, which lay on his head about as subtly as a dead deer on the front of a hunter's car.

In the middle of the meal my friend leaned forward and said quietly, "I have a secret to tell you. . . ." At this my giggles erupted and I had to bite my napkin as, with no insight into the way he was being perceived, he went ahead to tell me that his hair was not his own. I felt embarrassed at not being able to restrain my laughter, but he did not seem to notice at all. He went on talking, obviously enhanced in his own picture of himself, but without a clue as to the way the world looked at him.

I have thought often since then that we must all have behaviors and quirks that stand out just as clearly as that man's wig. And we may go along just as serenely self-deluded, our own truth clear to everybody but ourselves. It is easy not to see ourselves, and it would be a tragedy to miss at least a passing glance of what we are really like as we lead our lives. Only as we see this can we begin to deal again realistically with what we are still capable of being and what we are like now. It can help us look again on our possibilities for the future.

CHAPTER 10

━━━━◆━━━━

A time to love and a time to hate
A time of war
and a time of peace . . .

Waiting

Waiting must be important because there is so much of it in life. There is no shortage of in-between times, delays, or sudden interruptions for any of us. "Sorry, but your order won't be ready until next week. . . . Your plane has been delayed. . . . Is there anyplace I can wait around here? . . ." What is to be made of it all?

Some people have made waiting into an evil; they perceive it as a gap in existence that cannot be tolerated. We have all probably been tempted to think that way now and then. But very few of us have ever been able to do much about it. Oh, it is true that we can push things along in some areas of life, but hurried results are dissatisfying in their own way.

And the philosophies that urge us on to impulsive pleasure wear thin quickly. "Grab all the gusto you can get," we are told, but despite the efforts of several centuries of diligent drinkers, the satisfactions of life cannot be found in a cold beer.

There are more serious areas in which the delay of gratification has come to be regarded as heresy. *Don't wait for anything* is an easy slogan to claim, but in the important parts of life, it is almost impossible to live by. All kinds of things, from premarital sex to extramarital affairs, have been rationalized by this phrase. But, dizzied by the speed of life, we ask whether grabbing impulsively at existence can produce pleasure even for a fleeting instant. We already know that it cannot produce deep and lasting happiness.

We cannot overcome waiting anyway. There must be a deeper meaning for us here, something we need to understand in order to be fully human. Our days are so filled with waiting that it must have something to do with the meaning of life itself. Instead, if we can penetrate the mystery of waiting we may see the miraculous outlines of our existence more clearly.

Think for a moment of the waiting in our lives. What is it we wait for? And how deeply is this experience tied in with the meaning of hope? Indeed, hope would have no significance if waiting were not an essential ingredient in life. We wait for spring, yes, and for the mail to come. But, most of all, we wait for each other. It is a mystery, brushing by our face every day like a sudden unexplained leaf falling from a lifeless tree. Anybody who has ever loved knows how much waiting goes into love and how much waiting is important for its flourishing throughout a lifetime. Why is this? Why can't we have now, right now, what we need so desperately?

We cannot know the full explanation but we recognize that growth demands patient waiting. We have to give each other time to grow; that is the mysterious gift exchanged between those who wait. It creates the place in which we can wait just as it makes the environment right for growth itself. And nothing can substitute for it. There is no forced feeding in the most significant parts of life, no way to make people love us or to turn them mature overnight.

The secret begins to unravel when we understand these things: Waiting is not an unnecessary evil but an essential good. It is something we do for each other, hope come to full term, and through it we make ourselves present to others without making undue demands on them. We are with them and yet we let them move at their own pace. Is there anything more powerful than this invisible transaction? Probably not, because this kind of loving-waiting is what makes the world go round. And there is nothing harder to give than our waiting selves to those who need us. But there is life in the gift.

So we go through life, if we love at all, waiting often for each other, sometimes until we can look at something in the same way, sometimes until we can let each other freely look at things in quite different ways. There are times when we wait for others to heal, when we know that no approach of ours can help, when we can only stand by those who suffer with the small, patient gift of ourselves.

Indeed, there are moments when lovers hurt each other and cannot immediately regain the equilibrium of their relationship; they have to wait, sometimes in silence, while they regain their footing in each other's presence. We even have to wait for ourselves on some occasions, listening to the inner voices that tell us when we are ready or mature enough for the next step in our lives.

What would we miss if waiting were eliminated from life? The deepest love stories, for one thing. You cannot name one that is not filled with this strange but common mystery; waiting is worked into the design of any true lover's life. How could we ever find life if we were too impatient—too eager for a shallow species of gusto—ever to wait for it?

Not to be in the center

Pursuing happiness in America has been equated with being number one, with ending up on top no matter how one gets there. This often involves triumphing over one's competitors and living well or long enough to enjoy a sweet kind of revenge over one's enemies. Genuine happiness is hard to hold on to, but being number one—being so famous that nobody can ignore you—has seemed to many an adequate satisfaction to take the place of more substantial happiness.

The trouble with gaining the attention of everyone else comes from the amount of tension and unresolved conflict that goes into advertising one's accomplishments sufficiently in the first place. Some people have a wonderful talent for publicity, for turning even bad news about themselves to good advantage and handsome profit. There are, we recognize, those famous people we love or hate, the marvelous villains who gladly pay the price of a little dislike in order to enjoy a lot of acclaim. Only those who are Howard Cosells at heart just ask that the newspapers be sure to spell their names right no matter what they publish about them.

It is also true that many people get hooked on attention the way others do on drugs; it becomes a burden that is increasingly difficult to put down. They want to get rid of it but they cannot live without it. They are, as Alexander Pope said of Cromwell, "damn'd to everlasting fame." There is an ache in the soul of some celebrities, however, that is not totally disguised by what seems a glamorous life to most outsiders. They pound on the bars of their selves seeking for some kind of relief from the sentence they willingly accepted.

Director Mike Nichols, in an interview in *New York* magazine, reflected on some of his own experiences of fame. "There was this day that I went to this wise old analyst and said, 'I've gotta tell you, I really am tired of being Mike Nichols, get me out.' And then I asked him, 'Do you ever feel like this?' And he said, 'No, but long ago, I made a choice not to be at the center of things.'" A saying worth our meditation because it is a hard decision although it seems to guarantee peace.

What is the choice?

What, indeed, goes into the choice not to be at the center of things? Our motives can be obscure or mixed at times, and only the bravely honest allow themselves to feel the strong pull of their emotional crosscurrents.

It is possible, for example, for a person to make a choice out of fear. One might edge away from competition, and such hesitancy or uneasiness in a great man would be counted by historians as a flaw. The fear of losing makes many people stand back from the glare of the limelight. This does not bring them peace; such people are fearful even in the shadows.

Such a decision could be made because of some inner reluctance, some laziness of the spirit, the kind of passivity that is attributed sometimes to political leaders who stand next to greater power and never close their hands on it. "They didn't want it enough," observers say with a sneer. It may be a hard judgment, but standing still is not the same as making a choice to step back. Passivity is not the same as free choice.

The decision not to be at the center of things can also proceed from wisdom, through a not unpainful choice made only as we understand and weigh carefully the alternatives that are involved. A mature person, for example, may make such a choice in order to preserve values that might otherwise be destroyed. A husband and father may decide that time with his wife and children must be preserved along with rather than sacrificed for his professional advancement or he will destroy what he prizes most and fail in some of his most essential responsibilities. There are men and women in all walks of life who choose not to be at the center of things because they wish to share rather than dominate life. Such persons may give up more money for more of what they value humanly.

Less is more, the architects say, and in no place is this truer than in the heart of the decision to choose people rather than fame. Standing at the center of things—whether it is in medicine, law, a local union, or the religious life—can create whirling currents that sweep everything around us to destruction. There are too many unhappy people who stand in the limelight; it is only because it is so bright that one cannot see the wreckage of their personal lives scattered about them.

Is it copping out?

This is the most serious question, of course, because it is possible that in the name of other values, we may be avoiding responsibilities we should assume. Facing this is a big part of the pain for any person who is ever confronted with such a choice. Am I surrendering something that I should hold on to, giving up without ever realizing my full potential? Am I avoiding what I should confront? These are questions that are heard in many places these days. They are asked by persons who are restless in their own occupations and who wonder whether they should not abandon everything, sometimes including their families, in order to have a try at getting something else out of life. It may not seem like fame but it is certainly the kind of choice that puts one's own concerns first.

Sometimes the stories about such people—especially as they leave their families behind—oversimplify what is involved. One of the severest tests of our maturity, however, lies along that line where selfishness and the desire for authentic self-fulfillment somehow melt into each other.

Our culture emphasizes human potential, tempting individuals to discover their hidden powers and inviting them, in the self-hypnotizing slogans of supersalesmen and of accused swindler Glenn Turner, to "dare to be great." Self-fulfillment has been elaborately merchandised in the United States. It has come a long way from the magazine ads for body building and the mind power guaranteed by the Rosicrucians. The question that remains to be asked comes to this: After a certain period in life, are we still free to think only of ourselves and what we might do to improve our fortune or our fame?

Does maturity—and relationship to other persons—add dimensions that must be considered before we try to shoulder our way into the center of things? Too many families have been left behind with an ambiguous inheritance of personal uncertainty by those who have prized the front places of attention before everything else. Soul searching is not an easy venture. It is, however, required when we have grown to the state of not being able to think just of ourselves and our own needs. It is easy to seem to enrich ourselves only to impoverish those who are closest to us. It is difficult to give up some measure of attention from ourselves in order to make sure that we give enough of our attention to others. It is on the basis of such choices, however, that our true greatness really does rest. Greatness is a matter of the spirit, as it has always been, rather than an affair of bank accounts, sales records, or public applause.

Not just in big things

It may seem that these reflections only apply to those who are near to the inner circle of some profession. This is hardly so. We can be as eager to be the president of our local garden club as someone else might be to be president of the United States. We may crave attention with just as much longing as the famous person whose self-infatuation prevents him or her from realizing that other people really exist. Being at the center of things affects all worlds, large and small. The circle need be no larger than our own family.

We may profitably examine ourselves, asking whether, in fact, life does have to revolve around us. We get hints from the way the day runs and the way our convenience may become the element around which everything else must be scheduled. It may also become obvious in our conversations with our families or our friends, when we should be able to listen as well as speak. If we are always broadcasting our triumphs, making other people feel smaller as we make ourselves feel larger, complaining about our ills in a self-dramatizing way, then we may be cornering the market on attention and sympathy. It is a strange center of things to choose, but it is home base for a great many unhappy people.

Or does everyone have to tiptoe around us, paying court to us or leaving us plenty of room at the center of the stage? Have we become so distant that we do not even realize that we have estranged ourselves in a permanent way from the kind of closeness to others in which we discover and live the meaning of self-sacrificing faith? Self-sacrifice does not seem to have a very good name anymore; nobility has fallen on hard days.

A lover's question

It comes, at last, to be a question that only lovers can understand and, perhaps, only lovers can answer. What or whom do I love most of all? All too often we may discover that it is really ourselves we manage to smuggle into at least a tie for first place

in our affections. Our place, our feelings, our concerns are sometimes placed first in so subtle a way that we hardly notice we
have crowded everybody else out of our lives. Perhaps we only
recognize it in its ultimate effects, when we find that our affection for others has diminished or that we do not seem to have
good friends anymore. We may be very lonely and too involved
in our own concerns by the time we discover the truth.

Lovers choose every day not to be at the center of their own
lives and concerns. They choose instead to commit themselves
to others in a way that demands a steady kind of death and yet
provides an ever enlarging experience of life. As we give up the
center—knowing what we are doing and willingly paying the
cost—we may suddenly discover that we are at the center of
someone else's life, that love has enclosed us in that space of
intimacy where, giving, we have suddenly received; where, willing to lose everything, we have found everything instead.
Choosing not to be at the center of things is the test of whether
we love or only want to be loved; it is the unselfconscious sign
that true lovers give along with themselves, the sign of unself-
ishness in which we do not triumph but in which we find salvation.

Rejection

Does anything occur—or at least seem to occur—more often in
life than rejection? Do we dread anything more, or strive more
mightily to avoid anything, including plagues and earthquakes,
than this sharply painful experience? If there is, it has not been
named as yet.

The blade of rejection is dull and the cut across our souls is
jagged and a long time in healing. It is not something we like to
talk about. And that, of course, makes it worse, because rejection, like any wound, only closes if there is plenty of fresh air.
But we keep it even from ourselves, pulling down the curtain
and scurrying to hide, the way we did as children from the
lightning, in the darkness that does not make the danger disappear.

It may be related to the mysterious fact that we so often

conceal the best parts of our personalities. We protect the truth of ourselves out of fear that somebody will catch us in our weaknesses. Rejection is a special form of this because it builds its worst strength on ridiculing or, in subtle form, ignoring the efforts we count as most sincere and true. Rejection is powerful because it aims at our good intentions and our best efforts. Maybe we could agree if people just rejected our obvious weaknesses but we can only shudder when they won't accept our strength because that means they reject us altogether.

Some persons in the arts say that they never read the critics anyway. And Samuel Coleridge once noted that nobody ever raised a statue to a critic. It is not, however, the critics most of us worry about; it is each other. When we live close to each other we have a terrible power to hurt and reject each other, an almost awesome capacity to kill each other's spirit. And that is why we sometimes hide our best qualities—tenderness, for example—from those closest to us. We cover it up with blustering overmasculinity or some other psychological ruse in order to avoid the risk of having our better selves rejected.

But we get rejected anyway, no matter what we do, or how cleverly we disguise our hearts. It lies in the nature of life, and often enough, the more we worry about it, the more surely it comes to our door. Rejection is the worst of the bad weather of life and it seems to be in the forecast all the time. What are we to do about it? Say that it only hurts when we laugh, bite the bullet, or smile through our tears? Sometimes that is about all we can manage to do.

Part of rejection's power derives from our unwillingness to look it straight in the eye. We want to gaze in some other direction to distract ourselves from our pain. Suppose we looked more carefully into rejection for a change in order to discover its implications for our lives. Is there something to be learned here, a positive side to what seems the most negative of our experiences?

We might wonder, for example, whether we would ever be purified without it, or whether we would ever be able to see ourselves clearly unless we tasted rejection from time to time. After all, nothing reduces us to life-size like rejection. It may be painful, but it deprives us of our pretensions and our vanities as it burns away the dross of selfishness that crusts up on the edge of our souls. The scythe of rejection sweeps blindly across the lives of all of us, the just and the unjust alike. That's why we are all tempted on occasion to escape to the mountains or to a desert island in order to be safe from the assorted meanness of life.

We only know the worst pain of rejection if we are lovingly concerned for others; that is why lovers and parents are high on the list of those who feel it most keenly. It is impossible, both physically and emotionally, to reach out to others without yielding our protective guard at the same time. There is some affirmation of our effort to love in the experience of rejection. It is the hazard built into the effort, a special kind of dying that accompanies our best efforts to give life to others.

Jesus learned what life was all about, we might paraphrase, in the only way any of us ever does, through *taking the risks* of living rather than just talking about them. The experience of rejection allows us to see ourselves more clearly but it also tells us that we are on the right road. Denying rejection or trying to block it out of our lives may save us some of its pains, but it means that we have to stay on the outside of existence to do it. And that is a dead end indeed.

Setting ourselves up

What we must be careful about is the unconscious tendency to seek rejection. There will be no shortage of rejection anyway, so we should factor out all of it that is unnecessary as soon as we can. Courting rejection is something we have to watch for in ourselves and in others. Why?

We need to listen to our unconscious selves, especially if there is an overload of rejection in our lives. We can tell, for example, if we are always complaining about the way others mistreat us. Maybe we want it that way in order to punish ourselves for something, or in order to prove to ourselves that we are worthless and might as well give up on life. Americans need to watch themselves very carefully in this regard because they seem to enjoy feeling guilty so much. Give Americans somebody to make them feel guilty and they have a friend for life.

If we are not that way ourselves we may be on the other side of the equation; others may be pushing us to reject them for reasons they do not understand. People who want to be rejected usually manage to have their way, of course, but suppose we were patient or understanding enough to see beneath the maneuver. Suppose we refused to reject others, that we let them experience something quite rare, the powerful and loving understanding of their need to hide behind their own self-imposed rejection. That is the kind of loving response that is strong enough to bring them back to life, to help them drop their need for unnecessary suffering and unprovable guilt.

Making friends

Teaching people how to make friends may be *the* growth industry of North America. If there is a matter that concerns most human beings more than how to make and keep a good friend it has not been recorded as yet. But making friends is full of hazards. It is not surprising that some people have decided friendship is an experience whose emotional cost has become too inflated. Better, some think, to withdraw into the self and justify an isolated existence on some grounds or other. It doesn't make any difference what we say; all our reasons come down to attempts to protect hearts that break too easily.

This may even explain the current trend to downplay friendship and to exalt quick and easy sexual relationships; they may be ultimately unsatisfying but they are at least uninvolving. Not much human profit but no danger of great loss either. As a matter of fact, it is relatively easy to have sex with somebody else, even a stranger, but it is much more difficult to become a true friend to another person. Sex without relationship is less stressful than the personal investment demanded by friendship. If people treat each other as objects they don't have to deal with such things as learning about each other and making allowances or asking for and granting the forgiveness that, among other things, define friendship.

The bottom line comes to this: How are we going to go through life, as subjects or objects? Whether we lead a deep life depends on our understanding the difference between being a subject and an object. That is the key that unlocks life's best secrets—the difference between pleasure and happiness, force and freedom, making claims and setting others free.

In fact, in our personal lives and in our individual quests to find and to become better friends, we can only profit by pausing to reflect on the difference between . . .

Subjects and objects

Nobody wants to be an object in life. We can all tell when we are being treated this way. Half the protests of the present time —whether they are against assembly lines or all-digit dialing— are cries against being treated as objects. Sometimes we blame it on crowds and noise and the general impersonal character of a teeming civilization. The truth, however, is that we can be treated as objects by people close to us as well as by those at a distance, by friends as well as by strangers. We can, almost without thinking about it, treat others—and even ourselves—as objects. This is one of the chief ways we do it—by not thinking about it. It is from this very attitude that some of our greatest difficulties in friendship and love flow. Instead of making yet another list of the way others treat us as objects, we may examine the ways in which we do it to ourselves:

By using only part of ourselves. We deny ourselves a full subjective sense of our identity when we restrict the way we use our abilities in life. If, for example, we go through life overemphasizing our intellect, we may end up just thinking about life instead of living it fully. We may have an analysis of impressive intellectual dimensions for every situation but we will be fundamentally estranged from our true selves. The same thing can happen if we overemphasize our emotions, letting our feelings get out of balance so that we live impulsively. Feelings on the loose give rise to the heady enthusiasms of both revival religions and revolutionary crowds. We are less than subjects when we use only part of our personalities.

By expecting the worst. It is difficult for some persons to give up pessimism. It is their prized treasure and only as a last resort do they surrender their enthusiasm for bad tidings. They cannot imagine that anything good will happen to them or that other people may regard them favorably or want to do right by them. The arrival of a letter or telephone call makes them jump in anticipation that a new wave of sadness is about to crash over them. People who live this way claim that they are never really disappointed because they always expect the worst anyway. The truth is that they live lives of steady disappointment, stifling even the beginning of joy in their hearts. This is a cruel way of making objects of themselves.

By thinking and running our lives in the third person. It is surprising to find how many individuals actually do this. They never experience themselves directly. They seem instead to be standing like a coach on the sidelines, watching themselves and directing their moves from an approved play book. They remain at a distance from their own inner experience and so they speak about themselves as if they were referring to someone else. In revealing their motivation, for example, they say in effect, "A good husband does not act this way," or "A good mother does this or that," or "A good teacher acts in this fashion. . . ." This kind of separation from one's own experience—following guaranteed directions instead of one's own best instincts—is a sure way to treat oneself as an object.

By refusing to look at the full truth about ourselves. People do this whenever they distort their self-image, whether it is out of some false sense of humility or because they just feel generally uneasy about their own existence. Whatever it is, they seldom seem to give themselves a hearing or even much of a chance in life. It is strangely true that many of us hide the best thing about ourselves, the very thing that makes us most interesting and attractive. We do not allow ourselves even to look at these things and, for reasons that most of us cannot readily explain, we tend to mask the very strengths that are most important in making and keeping friends. This, in effect, denies us an opportunity to grow from within and keeps other people on the outside of us, limiting their view so that they can hardly be blamed if they cannot see enough of us to become our friends.

Think for a moment about how much energy some people put into obscuring what is a charming and attractive talent, whether it is for conversation, playing the piano, or being compassionate toward others. People restrain their strong points, perhaps because they sense the power in them and are afraid of losing control. They give up on the very things that make them unique in order to try to appear just like everyone else. Look around and you can see hundreds of thousands of people who dress alike, wear their hair and mustaches alike, crowding eagerly to the counters where they lose their individuality in what they think is its pursuit. They may be afraid that if they are not part of the great mass of midculture, they will be lonely. Sadly enough, they often end up lonely in the middle of this great throng. Perhaps this is because the people in it are hiding the best things that are in them, afraid that they will not hold up well in the light of day, or worried about the judgments of others.

Think for a moment of those who live their lives trying to meet the expectations that others make of them. They work very hard to fill a role designed by somebody else and they allow the dimensions of their personalities to be shrunk in order to fit. They are truly treating themselves as objects, processing their actions for approval by somebody else. Is it surprising that they are filled with yearning and loneliness?

Being a subject

Being a subject does not mean being merely subjective about life. If anything, it is a condition for breaking out of the kind of imprisonment that keeps us at a distance from ourselves and from others. When we are subjects rather than objects in life we have some sense of ourselves—the good and the bad—and we are not so uncomfortable that we cannot let this truth out. We can, in other words, stand undefended in an openness to what we are and to what we can still become in life. It is almost impossible to speak an "I" when we are estranged from our true selves. It is hard to be an "I" if we only deal with ourselves in the third person. And the beginning of friendship depends on becoming friendly enough with ourselves to treat ourselves as genuine subjects of existence. Some characteristics include:

Being a subject is built on the truth about our personalities. Many imagine that if the truth ever came out about themselves, it would not be acceptable. Finding out the truth about themselves, they seem to say, means finding out what is wrong with them. This, however, is a distortion, and if we are going to be fair with ourselves, we can at least admit the possibility that there are also good things lurking somewhere inside us. Sometimes we keep these hidden because admitting them would awaken us to further possibilities, to challenges of growth that we shy away from because of the effort they demand. We are subjects in life when we do not settle for what we have achieved so far. There is always something more, something richer to bring to life about ourselves.

This is not to say that all will be sweetness and light within our personalities. It will not all be bad, however, and what is imperfect about us does not deserve harsh judgments or punishments on our part. Indeed, an authentic experience of ourselves as subjects includes a willingness to identify clearly what is wrong inside us and to forgive ourselves for it. All forgiveness flows from our capacity to understand and to admit our own possibilities for evil. Denying them or trying to drive them underground does not help. Only we can welcome ourselves into the light with the forgiveness that resurrects rather than condemns us.

We are subjects when we can be aware of the many layers of our existence, when, in other words, we can break out of dealing with ourselves in the third person and can feel the depths of our identities. There is more music in us than we sometimes allow ourselves to hear. We may not understand it all, but that is hardly an argument for closing our ears to ourselves. Sensitivity to our own possibilities is an operational way of making an act of faith in ourselves and of giving ourselves both time and room to grow up from the inside. When we can hear and understand the many levels of our experience, we validate our own identity. We put a seal on our own presence in life, consolidating our very talents and making them available both to ourselves and to others. We should give at least as much understanding to ourselves as we sometimes seem willing to give to others. It is a way of expanding our own lives and the beginning of being a friend.

This is also a way of making room for ourselves so that we can test out our possibilities and our talents in life. We need room in order to make ourselves more fully available to those around us. We need enough space for the spontaneity that is such an important ingredient in all friendship and love. When we give ourselves room we no longer feel the pressure of living up to a redefined role or meeting the expectations of others. We no longer have to hide those things that may be most attractive about us. As we allow our true selves to emerge, we discover friendship in our life. Friendship with others builds on and reflects the basic friendship we have with ourselves.

What happens?

We soon discover that we are no longer hiding the best things about ourselves; we don't have to anymore. We are more comfortable with ourselves, and that makes other people more comfortable with us too. By such slow and almost imperceptible shifts we stop treating ourselves as objects and begin to sense the meaning of being subjects in life. We see ourselves in a new way and others do too. When we give ourselves a chance, when we allow the best side of ourselves to emerge, we find that we are in much better balance. We no longer need to worry so much about losing control or about people disliking us. We are freed from some of the defensive mannerisms that annoy others and keep them at a distance. This makes us more available to them as well. Where there was once a struggle to make ourselves presentable to others there is now a peaceful and less harried kind of presence. When we do not have to be like everybody else, we are much freer to be ourselves. This is part of the way in which we redeem ourselves and make ourselves available for friendship.

A strange thing happens. We are suddenly able to see other people more clearly because there is not nearly so much of ourselves in the way. We see others more as they truly are; we can respond to them rather than to some distorted picture we may have had of them. Nothing destroys friendship more than a person whose own ego fills all the available life-space. Then there can be no give or take, no real exchange of any kind because too much of one person is blocking the way. Terminal egocentricity kills even the possibility of friendship. The symptoms are clear: One person may insist too strongly on his or her own rights, keeping a careful record of who owes what and what favors are yet to be returned on the unbalanced mathematical tables of the heart. The justice in friendship has nothing to do with such bookkeeping. Friends work things out very approximately, very humanly, with each other; that is one of the ways they confirm each other as subjects in life.

When we have first made friends with ourselves we don't have to work so hard at winning the friendship of others. The conditions are right, in other words, for meeting people as they are and for having them meet us as we are. This is basic for the development of friendship. There is no manipulation and no force involved, no putting our best foot forward so awkwardly that we hide other things that are true and attractive about us.

The wonder of it

The wonder of discovering another person who can respond to us as a subject in life returns. There is a great mystery—and therefore an edge of true mysticism—in feeling the presence of someone who can reach gently into our own lives. Friendship is still one of life's great adventures, a never-ending one for people who know the difference between being subjects and objects and who do not get discouraged by the kind of hurts that may come along the way.

Friendship can then be more gentle and even-paced. It does not have to be hurried or brought quickly to some kind of conclusion in sexual relationships. There is great pressure on many young people to move past friendship and into sex before they even know each other. They therefore miss the miracle of meeting and learning to share things that is at the heart of life.

Friends do not hurry each other. They give each other both room and time—plenty of each in which to be separate and to be together. People remain friends because they remain distinct, because they respect each other's individuality and literally know how to let each other *be*.

Friends are always freeing each other for a richer taste of existence. It is only when they make too many claims or try to control each other that they kill friendship with the poison of jealousy and envy. People remain friends by giving each other away rather than clasping each other too tightly. And that, in the long run, is the secret of lasting friendship; it dies of barter, manipulation, and demands but it thrives when people give it away freely.

A meditation on truth

Truth, like gold for the forty-niners, may be where you find it. It seems to have lost some of its once-distinctive shape and, when last seen, was trailing down across the sky like a crippled dirigible, the subject rather than the master of the winds. No, truth does not seem to have the force it once had; we settle for pseudo-truths or for strangely worded promises from supposedly moral men that they will not lie to us. Truth exists the way an image exists on a photographic negative on which lights and shadows are shifted around; despite what we attempt to supply with our imagination, it does not deliver a satisfactory view of reality. Truth seems honored by a minimum deposit so that we get what we want without having to give too much of ourselves.

Truth emerges in a strange set of codes that include "No comment," "I will not confirm or deny it," and a dozen other statements that hang like steam above the cauldron of deception. "I did not talk *directly* to him," the man says as if to deny that he talked to him at all. Politicians are bad enough, but there are others who have done a great deal of damage to the nature of truth itself by all their manipulations of individual truths. "These were no ordinary criminals," humorist S. J. Perleman once wrote, "they were advertising men."

And, oddly enough, churchmen have been known to stretch the truth now and then. Theologians paved the way long ago, of course, with all their talk about "mental reservations," the lie that was not a lie, the falsehood that could be uttered for higher purposes. The example given in moral theology books was always that of the child who could tell the vacuum cleaner salesman that mother was not at home even though she was. This seems innocent enough; it only gets sinister in different and more important circumstances, although the same principle undergirds both.

The root trouble, a difficulty too simple to be glimpsed by some, is that the truth in these circumstances is just as simple and far more durable. And do we really know what we do to children by convincing them that it is all right to deceive in some situations and not in others? Whatever would be wrong with telling the vacuum cleaner salesman the truth? "My mother is at home now but she does not want to see you." Why not say directly and without rationalized convolutions what is really intended in the first place? Do we actually think the vacuum cleaner salesman doesn't know it?

And theologians have never even really agreed on the nature of a lie; they have always been good, for example, at discovering moral things that could be done in the midst of war. War seems to have been a major reason for not telling the truth. As a matter of fact, the very soul of war is falsehood and deceit, lie piled upon lie, and deception wed to disguise in a thousand darkened incarnations of evil. Better to admit the nature of war, that it is not fought by sportsmen and that it is devoid of romantic glamor, and that the worst lie of all is making it seem that it can ever be a good solution to human problems. It is far worse to overlook its nature and to see it as a theater in which we are permitted to deceive for the sake of victory.

One of the reasons that it is hard for modern people to have a clear view of sin is that we have blurred it so badly. We have tried to make falsehood a virtue against the heaving background of murderous war. Where does one discover the redeeming truth for the killing of the innocent, that by-product of the blood lust of which we seem never to have had enough?

And then there is the territory of the half-truth, the justified partial pilgrimage that brings gifts and takes them back at the same time. We seem to feel better if we tell part of the truth, letting that stand for the whole, and not letting ourselves see that falsehood does not understand such distinctions and that the more we barter with it the more it consumes us. Can it be this serious, we ask, this business of the truth? Are we not allowed some leeway, some room for self-defense, some way to purchase time against life's assaults on us?

No doubt we are, but we are much better off admitting the truth of our state to ourselves, that is, that we are deceiving, telling a species of lie rather than telling ourselves we are telling a species of the truth. It is always better to know what we are really doing, even when what we are doing is wrong, than to give it a label that it does not deserve and that can only confuse us. When we do the latter we never know where we stand and we may end up not being able to tell the difference between truth, half-truth, and falsehood. It all looks the same after a while.

Now we must allow some space for good intentions, for truths withheld or somewhat distorted for good reasons. We do not wish to hurt somebody else's feelings so we say maybe when we really mean no, or we say yes when we know we are going to transform it into no somehow or other later on. Ah, such noble intentions are quite understandable but they lead to grief in greater and lesser situations.

It has been learned, for example, that seriously ill people can stand learning the truth of their situation, that they deal better with the truth than with all the good-hearted deception in the world, and that, in a mysterious way, they sense the truth behind the lies anyway. This is because the truth is essential to their experience of themselves and they no longer have time for the luxury of denial.

The truth holds together even better in far less weighty situations; it is the only thing that holds together in any situation. And denying or exaggerating or telling some of the truth gets very confusing because it gets increasingly hard to remember what we have said to different people and we always run the risk of contradicting ourselves and revealing our diminished state anyway. There may be a virtue born of desperation or at least of necessity. It comes to life when we discover that telling the truth is easier and more satisfying than telling various versions of it.

We stumble into integrity because honesty really does prove to be the best policy; we no longer need remember what we told, or what part of what we told to whom, because we tell the same truth to everyone. It is only in the short run that distortions of the truth seem to save the feelings of others; in the long run such modifications of the truth hurt more than they help, in greater and lesser things, others and ourselves.

Then there are ways of recounting facts—accurate according to a certain measure—that may obscure rather than reveal the truth. Facts and the truth are by no means related. That is why, of course, we are rightfully wary of statistics, why, indeed, we must stand back and examine things carefully before we are sure that we have the truth of the matter.

Selective facts, for example, about a person's life hardly ever tell the truth about the person. The whole truth belongs to another realm of perception and recognition, a realm that may be far beyond the capacity of any overzealous investigative reporter either to understand or to enter. There are facts about all of us that we do not tell the complete truth of our being. Sometimes these are the only facts we allow ourselves to see; we are plagued by memories of our mistakes or our adolescent ways and we cannot perceive or give the proper respect to the many other good things that are true of us.

Self-esteem is the victim of the hanging judge in us who will look at the abridged factual evidence about us and refuse us a second chance. The truth about us is like an archaeological dig that needs sifting by those who can understand its layers and who do not rush to judgment too soon. The truth demands time and patience and the sensitivity of a novelist rather than the punchy expression of a headline writer.

Telling the truth about ourselves is much harder than telling the facts. The facts are, in some ways at least, easy and they can be rattled off like name, rank, and serial number. But the truth, the seven-storied truth, is delivered through the way we live. It is not even secured by the compulsion to confess that is so widespread in our culture, the infected mood of late-night talk shows and some so-called therapy group confrontations. We only tell the truth by living the truth, by being truthful in the most profound and existential way.

There is power in the moment of truth because it is the instant in which we process our existence, in which we give an answer to the Scriptural question, How can a man be born again? Men and women are born again whenever they reveal the truth of themselves; there is more of them alive in the moment after they have told the truth than there was in the previous moment. They make the word flesh, and such is its power that they grow through this very act and those touched by their truth also grow.

There is an almost blinding force in the truth that is revealed in this human manner. Think, for example, of the power in the truth told to us by a child. For here we are witness to the elemental strength that radiates from a truthful person. Watch little boys or girls as they look us straight in the eye and tell us, not what we want to hear necessarily, but the rock bottom truth of their own experience. It is not easy for them to admit it, perhaps, but something occurs in that instant of guileless revelation. They are more alive and so are we.

The truth retains this power. Perhaps men have turned away from it because they know this power and they are afraid to face it because they sense that it will make demands on them which cannot be met by rationalizations and denials, by long explanations and half-truths. Perhaps we have chosen the chains of delusion because we are not ready, perhaps not yet mature enough, to accept the promise that the truth will make us free.

Hard times for friendship

Among those who have had something to say on the subject of friendship we find the rich and the powerful as well as the wise and the analytic. First, let us consider the rich and the powerful —which is like saying first, the bad news, except that the wise and the analytic can hardly be classed more optimistically.

The rich and the powerful. Take, for example, Bernie Cornfeld, whose travels from one pleasure dome to another with a retinue of vacant-looking young women has been closely chronicled in the news magazines. Bernie is quoted as saying, "I don't have huge expectations from any kind of friendship. In the final analysis, we are all pretty much alone."

Turn then to another rich man, the celebrated Jean Paul Getty, featured in yet another magazine under the heading, "World's Richest Man Lives in Elegant Isolation." Getty, concluding that women are attracted by failure and repelled by a man's drive to succeed, says, "You rarely see a successful man with a happy marriage . . . but you have to decide what you want and I haven't regretted putting business first."

And a well-known American churchman protested to a recent interviewer that he could not have friends. "I wouldn't say that I had any true close friends and yet everybody is my friend. No close friends, though. I don't have the time. No best friend . . . I simply don't have the time to have what you'd call a 'best friend' or a 'close friend'; or however you choose to say it. . . . But in my position as a religious leader, there is no need for any best friend. Everyone is my friend."

It may sound stuffy to observe that Scrooge used the same line of reasoning until the ghost appeared, but there they are, the rich and the powerful: Friendless by their own admission, their priorities intact and their hearts presumably at peace. The point may be that power can substitute to some extent for friendship. Power is appealing; it is like insulation against loneliness but it is not much of a substitute for friendship. "If you have power," a famous man once told me, "you don't need friends." Yes, but if you have friends you don't need power quite so much either.

The wise and the analytic. It is certainly fashionable to say that we are all ultimately alone, as far, finally, from each other's hearts as the nearest stars to ours. So what is the difference anyway? The less you make of love the better, the argument goes, and the easier it is on the heart.

What, then, do the wise and analytic have to say about friendship and love? There may be nothing worse for the subject of tenderness than to let the social scientists dig into it. They sometimes remind me of an old professor I once had who would chew on a subject with the slow but determined enthusiasm of an old tramp at a flophouse Thanksgiving dinner. He would chew it this way and that, grinding it with his philosophical-theological molars until what began as something interesting was gradually transformed into something boringly dull and finally unbearably bland. This man did not teach; he compacted the stuff of life into dry, antiseptic trash as insubstantial as ashes. But, back to the social scientists.

In a recent symposium on the subject of love, the following observations were made by some of the participants:

The psychologist advised the audience that romantic love "is too demanding on both the lover and the loved." He quoted, with apparent admiration, the cynical remark of H. L. Mencken: "Love is the delusion that one woman differs from another."

The sociologist said that romantic love "is predicated on a power-based relationship" and is that love "which has been corrupted by an unequal balance of power." If you begin using that vocabulary about love it is hard to see how you could say anything good about it.

The anthropologist, however, concluded in this grave new world fashion: "Love may be like a crutch, impeding the development of new social forms so important for the development of a better and more satisfying human condition and society of the future."

And, we might conclude, these are the people who are supposed to help us find our way in this confusing world. It is fortunate, of course, that we still have poets in the land to remind us of what is truly important about life and who know that what goes on in the heart of our relationships with each other must be treated sensitively if we are going to understand it better. What, in fact, do we do to friendship when we say that there really is no time for it in life and that other things, like business, must come first? And what do we do to friendship when we overanalyze it, using special vocabularies so that it becomes unpleasant even to think or talk about?

We are talking about something when we put friendship aside for business or talk about it in deadly scientific terms, yet this is not friendship as most people understand it. Nothing warm or illuminating there. Such reflections dress our souls in mourning because they kill our spirit and, in the name of making life more manageable, make it unbearable instead.

Friends always say yes: true or false?

As if the young have not already had enough misleading philosophies preached to them by adolescent elders, a new notion, made more dangerous because it affects the central experience of friendship, is now highly popular on campuses and almost anywhere that the hard rock music plays. There is no need to lecture young people about this, of course; they suffer enough lectures, as we all do, about the way we should behave. It is vital, however, to listen to what is going on in the struggle young people go through to understand love and friendship and to help them sort out what is deep from so much that is shallow.

The young are made more vulnerable by their generosity and their eagerness for closeness with others. That is why they are prey to the latest faddish words on how friends treat each other.

And the latest reads this way: *you always do what your friend asks of you.*

That notion is just hazy enough to be enormously attractive to persons ready to prove their love or, perhaps more accurately, to reveal their need for love of others. Following this maxim leads individuals to put themselves and their plans in second place; if your friend calls, drop everything and respond because your friend's needs are everything. You are just not much of a human being unless you are ready to throw your own schedule overboard in order to do what your friend wants.

Now there is something in this, something of the responsiveness of real love; but hardly everything that is connected with friendship as it is found—and as it flourishes—in real life is like that. That is because friendship has a context that cannot be disregarded. Love grows in the real world and the real world cannot be totally ignored or love will not last for long. Why might we hesitate to endorse a principle that seems so noble?

Loving ourselves and others

First of all, any relationship we have reflects and depends upon our relationship with ourselves. The model for loving our neighbors is always based on the way we love ourselves. So we cannot ignore our own persons in any relationship without immediately making it lopsided and, in the long run, something very different from our true friendship. Leave ourselves—our obligations, our needs, our other relationships—leave these out in the name of always doing what our friend wants and we harm ourselves. And we cannot harm ourselves without at the same time harming the person we call a friend. Always throwing our time or rights away to do what a friend wants undoes friendship itself because it introduces such an imbalance into the situation. We cannot, in other words, treat ourselves poorly and think that we are really treating anybody else well. Just inspect the distorted relationships of this kind that already exist: the babied partner whose chances of becoming an adult are thereby lessened; the totally self-sacrificing partner who is destroyed because there is hardly an edge of life left to cling to.

This philosophy also ignores the truth that friendship and love flourish only where the persons remain separate and distinct from each other. They don't blend into romantic mush where their identities are irretrievably lost. The magic—and the long-lasting wonder—of genuine friendship and love depends on precisely the opposite happening. When human beings have clearly defined identities they are capable of a relationship. They will not get lost in the mire of unrecognized needs; they will not trap or be trapped by emotions they do not understand. People who love each other are able to do this because they respect the distance between each other and because they leave plenty of room for each to be separate. Because they do this they are able to live in a deeply joyful way. They are far enough apart to allow the lightning of love to leap across the space between them and close enough to be able to see each other whole. That means that the needs of one can never totally predominate without imperiling the very foundations of friendship. It is not easy for anybody to learn the lessons of the love that respects rather than obliterates differences. Yet it is impossible to learn if we begin with the shaky premise that only the needs of the other count. *Unconditional surrender,* in the opinion of many, made the second World War bloodier and more deadly than it needed to be; it is not a good principle in friendship either.

The dangers of friendship

If we always give in to the needs of somebody else we can do a lot of damage to our personal and professional lives. Young people, following this philosophy to the extreme, can flunk out of school without really trying. Love does not take away all the private space of another's life; it is a counterfeit when it refuses to acknowledge the overall context of reality. This is particularly tragic for the young who may easily have their generosity manipulated into disaster for them. What better maxim for an unconverted male chauvinist, for example, than that his needs must always come first? No need just to pick on men, of course, but add this aphorism in with the other shallow rationalizations that abound—As long as nobody gets hurt or As long as nobody else knows—and a great deal of unnecessary hurt will surely follow.

The results of an excessive application of this notion can include the pain that goes with being used or disappointed in love; the wounds are sometimes invisible but the scars on people's lives are not. Individuals who are the victims of this philosophy may also find that a steady diet of always giving up everything for the other may slowly, almost imperceptibly, build up a tremendous store of resentment in themselves. They may not want to admit it, not even to themselves, but such accumulated anger is also destructive of what they want most in the way of happiness and friendship.

Worse still, however, is that people who buy this notion are automatically on the outside of the experiences that are most important for the survival of love. What need for *understanding*, if one always has to give in to the other? What need for *tenderness*, if everything goes one way in these relationships? If life and love were so simple, we would never need to refine our *sensitivity* to each other; we would never have to break out of ourselves and meet anew somewhere in between our egos. We would never really have to *believe* in each other or reach out toward each other in *hope*. Nor would we ever have the satisfaction of experiencing *resurrection* together because we retain the life-giving power of our distinct personalities. Perhaps worst of all, we would never *surprise* and *delight* each other; there would be no way in which this could happen because the relationship would be so bent out of shape that we could never see more of each other all the days of our lives. The richest and best mysteries of love would elude us just as they always do when somebody comes up with a smooth-sounding but deceptive code of friendship.

On leaving room for love

The world, Chesterton once wrote, is as "wild as an Old Wives' Tale," a judgment few of us would dispute, especially when the world starts talking about love. It has never gotten tired of the subject but it has never been quite sure what to think or how to express it either. Where, for example, is love to be found? There are as many opinions about this as there are maps locating wreckage-held treasures on the ocean floor. And explorers are constantly outfitting romantic expeditions to search out the sources of love that they know are there if only, yes, if only they find the right spot.

Love is sometimes sought as though it existed like a measurable quantity; if you are lucky at one of the garage sales of life you may purchase a hamper of it and be dazzled when you open it by the smell of ginger and other sweet perfumes. You will find love, the old dream tells us, if you look hard enough and bargain sharply enough for it. It is the gold of existence for those who reach out and make it their own. And so the search goes on with lonely people wondering, like once-lucky prospectors, if they will find it this time out . . . on a cruise, or in a single's bar, or deep in the look of a stranger's eyes.

For others, love is the outcome of magic. It can be made to appear out of nothing; the conjurer's hat snaps sharply and love comes alive like a brace of furry rabbits. All one need do is master the trick of knowing the right words or incantations, by shooting the starry houses of the zodiac like a navigator of the emotions. Love, in this view, comes to those who wish hard enough, to those who wait for deliverance by fate or alchemy. What is the truth about love? Does it belong to the measurers or the sorcerers? Does one grab for it or just long for it?

Love, of course, has no mass although it is filled with power. It is not scattered like bullion awaiting the serendipiter's pick, but neither is it as insubstantial as a wistful adolescent's dream. Love does not occupy space although it can fill us to the brim. It leaves traces but these cannot be plotted on a graph. We know it exists but we cannot make an act of the will or utter secret words that force it into life. We can easily get our ideas of love mixed up and as a result find ourselves frustrated and sometimes heartbroken. Setting out to win somebody else's affection, for example, is as painful a journey as any we are ever likely to undertake. Wishing for love never does make it appear, but too much wishing against an empty, moonlit sky can surely make us lonelier than we need be.

What can be done about it?

Oddly enough, we learn that although love does not occupy physical space we still must leave plenty of room for it in life. It does not respond to the swift gestures of the magician but it trails off into mystery nonetheless. Love, like a freshly kindled flame, needs air; it cannot be crowded lest it be smothered to death. How, then, leaving aside magic and mathematics, can we be sure it will have ample space in which to grow?

Love is a creature of the edges and gaps of life more than of anywhere else. We fall in love, for example, when we suddenly see what is different about each other, when we glimpse the truth of personality that burns, like the leaping flames of the sun, beyond the edges of our everyday presentation of ourselves. Others love us when we allow them to see those unpredictable and necessarily imperfect features that we sometimes cover up "in order to make a good impression." It is difficult for people to see what is spontaneous about us when we are buttoned down and polished up, when, in effect, we are alienated from the least affected aspects of ourselves.

Charm is a word that has suffered from being applied to superficial and artificial ways of attracting attention. We can be charmed by con men or politicians, and most of us have an early-warning system against their wiles. But real charm is a quality of innocence and goodness and it takes away rather than activates our defenses. Charm is what shows through when we don't try to seal all the gaps in our personalities; it is what others can see when we are unselfconscious and are not trying to impress them. Love follows on such revelation and there is no sure way to prepare for it except by not preparing. The only thing we can do is leave room—enough living space—for love to find its way into our lives. Love has no mass but it grows only in the space where the truth about us shows through.

The price

The price of being alive is that of bearing witness to constant, continuing, inevitable change; living deeply means sticking with people during changing times and not giving up on the elements of self-investment—believing, hoping, and loving—that deliver meaning to our existence. It is better to have loved and discovered how hard it is to keep on loving than never to have loved at all.

The deadly enemy

And we need to leave room for love all the way along the path of existence. Strangely, however, people turn back to tricks in their efforts to preserve or, at times, to find new love. They do this out of fear that they will lose love. That fear is love's most deadly enemy. People are afraid that others will not like them or that they must always please others in a certain way. The more they invest themselves in such activities the further they drift away from their real selves and even from the very possibility of love.

Being perfect and getting it right all the time are notions that leave no room for love. What need for love, what need for faith or hope either, if we could master our behavior and always deliver that which is without seam and beyond question? There would be little need for love—and no room, surely—if all we had to do was present ourselves in the current styles, our genuine personalities swathed beyond reproach or recognition in the latest acceptable fads. That is the fate that awaits people who dote on how-to-do-it books, on the gimmickry of an age that has attempted to bring technology to interpersonal affairs.

Believe

Believing takes something more active than just saying yes to a certain formulation of creeds. It demands a continuing investment of ourselves in everybody and in everything around us. It is a virtue of involvement with the universe because it establishes a living contact between us and those who share existence with us.

Most of us remember the childish magical notion that if we didn't do something—hold our breath or stand perfectly still—the world would shatter into fragments around us. We have put that idea away, but its memory stirs us to thought. The world will not fall apart if we do not believe. Something else will happen. We will collapse in on ourselves like ancient exhausted stars. Refusing to believe, we refuse our first contact with the reality all around us; we squirm away from the events that humanize us by drawing on but in no way diminishing our existential reserves.

To believe brings us into being; it is the activity that processes our existence because it makes the first connections between ourselves and others. There is something reciprocal in the way others believe in us and our learning to believe in the same way in others. Belief is a building block of our humanity on which everything else finally stands. Belief involves us in reality by awakening us to the possibilities of existence. It is not an activity that looks backward but one that addresses the future, making us aware of what we can become as human beings. Belief also plunges us into the mystery of what others can become because of our human presence to them.

Believing is one of those activities that cannot be rehearsed. We don't *practice* belief. We do it or we don't understand it at all. The things that humanize us are not things we work ourselves up to; they are not once-in-a-lifetime activities. They are the things we are involved in all the time. We either give ourselves to them or we miss an important part of our existence.

Hope

Hoping is in this same order of vital experience in which there are no time-outs. It is another part of the way in which we get more deeply into life itself by learning to reach out toward others. Hope builds on the understanding that we always make a difference to each other. Hope is the virtue that pivots on the reality of our relationships to each other and it lives in any action in which we truly reach out toward persons for their sake. Hope recognizes that the way we make ourselves present to others—of whether we are with them or not—gives shape to our lives. It isn't just what we do or say when we are with them. There is another link, the strength and sustenance of hope, that helps us keep going. This reality challenges the contemporary thought that we can do anything as long as we don't hurt somebody else or as long as nobody else knows what we are doing. Hope reveals that invisible web of reality in which we are continually enlarging or taking something away from each other's spirit. Hope says we always make a human difference and that we do this even in the smallest actions of the day.

This is why there is so much energy in hope that is as strong and as invisible as the wind; we either make ourselves available to other persons—we are with them, for them wholeheartedly, or we are, in effect, against them. We are either awake to each other, in other words, or we miss what is exciting and challenging about being human.

It should not surprise us that a small amount of hope goes a long way. Hope does not need to be administered in large doses. It has its best effects when it is a steady and consistent commitment of our spirit to that of another. Hope is communicated when we pay attention, when we really listen, for example, to somebody else. This is hope in action because such active listening means that we are open to another's existence; whenever we do this, something momentously humanizing occurs.

Hoping, however, does not just do something to those around us. We cannot hope, even in the simplest circumstances, without making something happen to ourselves at the same time. Through hope we insert ourselves more deeply into the mystery of existence; we feel what life asks of us but in the same moment we know what we also get in return.

Love

Love is sadly elusive for many persons. It is often talked about as though it were something outside of ourselves. That is why people are always asking where they can find it or how they can be sure that it is everything they expect it to be or that it will last through a lifetime. They would bite it, as they would a coin, to be sure it was not counterfeit. And so people consider themselves lucky if they find and can hold on to love.

Love lies in the possibility of our response to those around us; it is not a gift floating just beyond our fingertips in the air. Love gives us the energy to do more than just seek nourishment from life. Love alerts us to other persons and to the fact that we are not just scattered loosely like dice on a gaming table. It is not just a matter of fate where we land in relationship to each other. Neither are we destined to swell like microscopic animals bumping and sliding off each other without any consciousness of our movements together.

Love belongs to those who understand that they are not meant to be blind to each other's features. Love is not blind at all. It depends on our willingness to see deeply into each other and, therefore, at the same time to see more deeply into ourselves. Love is at the very heart of the trembling mystery of revelation. It is indeed the virtue for people on a journey. The capacity to love matches the fact that we haven't finished our journey yet. It also helps us recognize that we travel together and that, in the long run, there is nothing that we can do all by ourselves.

We find ourselves together and love's mystery is expressed in the fact that the more we make room for others the more space we find for ourselves. Love doesn't do anything for us unless we are ready to do something for others. It tells us that life is not about winning but about sharing and that real wealth is not about holding on to things but about knowing how to let them go.

What are we supposed to do in life anyway? We are supposed to enter into these experiences and the opportunity comes with every day. People who believe and hope and love are doing the things that alone deliver to us a sense of being alive. Through the experience of incarnation and through a thousand deaths we lay hold of the mystery of life.